The Science of Karma

As expounded by the
Gnani Purush Dada Bhagwan

Originally Compiled in Gujarati by :

Dr. Niruben Amin

Publisher : Mr. Ajit C. Patel
Dada Bhagwan Aradhana Trust
Dada Darshan, 5, Mamta Park Soc,
B/h. Navgujrat College, Usmanpura,
Ahmedabad-380014,
Gujarat, India.
Tel. : +91 79 3983 0100

Price   : Ultimate humility and the intent that
'I do not know anything'!

Printer   : **Amba Offset**
B -99, Electronics GIDC, K-6 Road
Sector -25 , Gandhinagar - 382044.
Gujarat, India.
Tel. : +91 79 39830341

Trimantra
(The Three Mantras)

Namo Vitaraagaya
I bow to those who are absolutely free from all attachment and abhorrence

Namo Arihantanam
I bow to those living Ones who have annihilated all internal enemies of anger, pride, deceit, and greed

Namo Siddhanam
I bow to those who have attained total and final liberation

Namo Aayariyanam
I bow to all the Self-realized masters who impart Knowledge of liberation to others

Namo Uvazzayanam
I bow to those who have received the Knowledge of the Self and are helping others attain the same

Namo Loye Savva Saahunam
I bow to all saints everywhere who have received the Knowledge of the Self

Eso Pancha Namukkaro
These five salutations

Saava Paavappanasano
Destroy all demerit karma

Mangalanam cha Saavesim
Of all that is auspicious

Padhamam Havai Mangalam
This is the highest

Om Namo Bhagavate Vasudevaya
I bow to all who have attained the absolute Self in human form

Om Namah Shivaaya
I bow to all human beings who have become instruments for salvation of the world

Jai Sat Chit Anand
The Awareness Of The Eternal Is Bliss

Who is Dada Bhagwan?

In June 1958, around 6 o'clock one evening, amidst the hustle and bustle of the Surat railway station while seated on a bench, 'Dada Bhagwan' manifested completely within the sacred bodily form of Ambalal Muljibhai Patel. Nature revealed a remarkable phenomenon of spirituality! In the span of an hour, the vision of the universe was unveiled to him! Complete clarity for all spiritual questions such as, 'Who are we? Who is God? Who runs the world? What is karma? What is liberation?' etc. was attained.

What He attained that evening, He imparted to others through his original Scientific experiment (*Gnan Vidhi*) in just two hours! This has been referred to as the *Akram* path. *Kram* means to climb up sequentially, step-by-step while *Akram* means step-less, a shortcut, the elevator path!

He, himself, would explain to others who Dada Bhagwan is by saying, "The one visible before you is not Dada Bhagwan. I am the *Gnani Purush* and the One who has manifested within is Dada Bhagwan who is the Lord of the fourteen worlds. He is also within you, and within everyone else too. He resides unmanifest within you, whereas here [within A. M. Patel], He has manifested completely! I, myself, am not God (*Bhagwan*); I also bow down to the Dada Bhagwan who has manifest within me."

❖   ❖   ❖   ❖   ❖

4

The Current Link to Attain Self-Realization

After attaining the Knowledge of the Self in 1958, absolutely revered Dada Bhagwan (Dadashri) traveled nationally and internationally to impart spiritual discourse and Self-realization to spiritual seekers.

During his lifetime itself, Dadashri had given the spiritual power to Pujya Dr. Niruben Amin (Niruma) to bestow Self-realization to others. In the same way, after Dadashri left his mortal body, Pujya Niruma conducted spiritual discourses (*satsang*) and imparted Self-realization to spiritual seekers, as an instrumental doer. Dadashri had also given Pujya Deepakbhai Desai the spiritual power to conduct *satsang*. At present, with the blessings of Pujya Niruma, Pujya Deepakbhai travels nationally and internationally to impart Self-realization as an instrumental doer.

After Self-realization, thousands of spiritual seekers prevail in a state free from bondage and dwell in the experience of the Self, whilst carrying out all their worldly responsibilities.

❖❖❖❖❖

Note About This Translation

Param Pujya Dadashri's spiritual discourses were in the form of answers to questions asked by spiritual aspirants. These discourses were recorded and compiled into books.

Dadashri had said that it would be impossible to translate His *satsangs* and the Knowledge about the Science of Self-realization word-for-word into English, because some of the meaning would be lost in the process. Therefore, in order to understand precisely the *Akram* Science of Self-realization, He stressed upon the importance of learning Gujarati.

Dadashri did however grant His blessings to translate His words into English and other languages so that spiritual seekers could benefit to a certain degree and later progress through their own efforts. This book is not a literal translation, but great care has been taken to preserve the essence of His original message.

For certain Gujarati words, several English words or even sentences are needed to convey the meaning, hence many Gujarati words have been retained within the English text for better understanding. At the first instance in your reading, the Gujarati word will be italicized followed by a translation explaining its meaning in round brackets. Thereafter, the Gujarati word will be used in the text that follows. This serves a two-fold benefit; firstly, ease of translation and reading and secondly, it will make the reader more familiar with the Gujarati words, which is critical for a deeper understanding of this spiritual Science. The content in square brackets provides further clarity in English which is not present in the original Gujarati content.

❖ ❖ ❖ ❖ ❖

Special note to the reader

The Self is the Soul (*Atma*) within all living beings.

The term pure Soul is used by the *Gnani Purush* for the awakened Self, after the *Gnan Vidhi*. The word Self, with an uppercase 'S', refers to the awakened Self which is separate from the worldly-interacting self, which is written with a lowercase 's'.

Wherever Dadashri uses the term 'we', 'us', or 'our', He is referring to Himself, the *Gnani Purush*.

Similarly, the use of You or Your in the middle of a sentence, with an uppercase first letter, or 'You', 'Your' in single quotes at the beginning of the sentence, refers to the state of the awakened Self or *Pragnya*. This is an important distinction for the correct understanding of the difference between the awakened Self and the worldly-interacting self.

Wherever the name 'Chandubhai' is used, the reader should substitute his or her name and read the matter accordingly.

The masculine third person pronoun 'he' and likewise the object pronoun 'him' have been used for the most part throughout the translation. Needless to say, 'he' includes 'she' and 'him' includes 'her'.

For your reference, a glossary of all the Gujarati words is either provided at the back of the book or available on our website at:

http://www.dadabhagwan.org/books-media/glossary/

While reading this English translation, if you feel there is any contradiction or discrepancy, then it is the mistake of the translators and the understanding of the matter should be clarified with the living *Gnani* to avoid misinterpretation.

❖❖❖❖❖

PREFACE

Countless unimaginable and unexpected events such as plane crashes, bombings, fires, earthquakes and tornadoes causing innumerable deaths, have been known from television and newspapers! Many people have met their death in accidents or from diseases and hunger. Many have died right after birth and many have committed suicide. There have also been dark scandals involving preachers. At the same time the evolved souls of saints, devotees, and Gnanis (Self-realized) have been experiencing the bliss of Self (*nijananda*). When scandals arise, people become curious. Why are babies born disabled? One does not find any consolation. People's minds are silenced because they cannot resolve and understand the true nature and laws of karma. What is karma? How does one bind or accumulate karmas? Where does it all begin? What was the very first karma? How can one be liberated from karma? Can one avoid experiencing karma? Is God the doer of karma or is he the instigator behind them? What comes after death? Who binds all these karmas? Who experiences these karmas, the *Atma* (Soul) or the physical body?

What do our people call karma? According to people in general, karma means going to work, performing meritorious deeds, charity, and religious activities. The Self-realized however, call these '*karmaphala*' (resultant karma) instead of karma. The gross karmas, which can be seen and experienced through the five senses, are all *karmaphala* or discharge karmas. That which was charged in the past life is being discharged in this life. It is manifested and becomes visible. The karmas performed at the present time are done at the subtle level. The charging point is very difficult to grasp or recognize.

A businessman, pressured by his relatives, donates five *lakh* rupees to a charity trust, while his friend asks, "Why did you donate money? Don't you know that they are all thieves and embezzlers?" The businessman tells his friend that he knows

8

that. If he had his way, he would not have given even five rupees, but he was forced to donate the money due to pressure from the chairman who happens to be his relative. Now that he has donated five *lakh* rupees, people praise him for his generosity, which in fact was his discharge karma. What did he charge? He has charged karma by saying that he would not have given even five rupees! On a subtle level he charges exactly the opposite, so that in his next life he will not be able to give even five rupees. A poor man, donates five rupees to the same charity and says that if he had five *lakh* rupees, he would give it all. Because he gives the money heartily, in his next life he will be able to donate five *lakh* rupees. So, whatever you see externally, is all the fruit of actions, but on a very subtle level the seeds being sown cannot be discerned. Only if you have inward vision (*antarmukh drashti*), can you see this. Now, is it necessary to spoil one's intent and emotions after such an understanding?

The karmas that one binds, such as 'to eat, drink and be merry, are called *sanchit* karmas, or accumulated karmas. Such karmas are stockpiled at a subtle level and when they are about to ripen and give fruits, a person is inspired to eat unhealthy food and when he is done eating it is called *prarabdha* karma (fate). This in turn gives a final result, which is the effect of effect so that he may end up having dysentery and become sick. That is *kriyamana* (exhausted resultant) karma.

Param Pujya Dadashri shows us that *Vyavasthit Shakti* includes the principles of karma. Karma is only a small fraction of *Vyavasthit*, it doesn't include the total process. Karma belongs to *Vyavasthit* but *Vyavasthit* does not belong to karma. Karmas are carried on in a subtle form as seeds from the past life. However, it does not end there. When the karma starts producing fruits, (i.e., trees grow from the seeds) so many circumstances are required. The seed becomes a mango tree and one can receive mangoes. This process involves many other evidences such as, soil, water, sunshine, fertilizer, heat

9

and time. Dadashri has explained beautifully, that these are the fruits of karma. The seeds of karma are active at the very subtle level.

Many people ask how the first karma was bound. Did the body come before the karma? Did the chicken come before egg? It is all the same. In reality, there is no such thing as the first karma in the world. Karma and *Atma* have existed throughout time without a beginning or an end. Karmas are charged atoms. The *Atma* is the living or conscious *tattva* (element). Both *tattvas* (*atma* and matter) are always separate. A *tattva* is an eternal element. How can there be a beginning to that which is eternal? All karmas are charged because of the union of the living (*chetan*) and non-living (*jada*). It is the seed karma (cause or charge karma), which gives the fruit of karma (effect or discharge karma) in the next life. Karmas produce circumstances that by nature are temporary. Union is followed by separation. Circumstances come and go, giving rise to various stages of existence and events. When the wrong belief, "I am this and this is mine," arises it results in the visible and tangible worldly life. If one understands this mystery then there is only the *Shuddhatma* (Pure Soul) and *sanyog* (circumstance). Owing to the lack of such understanding we use the gross language of *prarabdha* and call it fortune, fate, or destiny, etc. The science however tells us this much, that if we remain separate from the evidences, then we can stay in the *Atma* and only then, karma does not exist.

How does one bind karmas? Karmas are bound by the subtle belief of doership in any action.

What is doership *bhaav*? When someone else does the karma and one believes that "I am doing it" is called doership-*karta bhaav*.

Why does the doership, *karta bhaav* originate? It originates because of *ahankar* (ego).

What do we call ego? The ego is the belief, "I am that," when truly one is not that. When the Self is identified wrongly, it is ego. It is ego when one believes, "I am Chandubhai,", because here one identifies himself with his name and body. "I am this body, I am her husband." In reality, one is the Pure Soul, but he is not aware of this real identity. Because the person does not have this awareness, he identifies himself as 'I am Chandulal' and 'I am this body.' This belief is ignorance and it is because of this ignorance that karmas are bound.

If you renounce the identification with the body, then you are not the doer of karmas and neither are you the enjoyer or sufferer of these karmas. That is the ultimate essence of *dharma*.
~Shrimad Rajchandra

If you are an embodied soul, or *jiva* then Lord Hari is the doer. If you are *Shiva*, the primordial Soul, then that is the true essence (meaning you are not the doer). ~ Akha Bhagat.

When one identifies with, "I am Chandulal," it is called *'jiva dasha'* (embodied soul). When one becomes aware of the Gnan that, "I am not Chandulal, but I am *Shuddha Atma* (Pure Soul) in reality," that is called *'Shiva pada'*. One is *Shiva*. The *Atma* is *parmatma,* whose natural state is devoid of all mundane actions. The *Atma* by nature has no doership. It is the Gnani who is constantly aware of, "I am the Self," and "I am not the doer of anything," and therefore he does not bind new karmas. The old discharge karmas mature, give fruit, and are exhausted.

The seeds of karmas are sown in the past life and give their fruits in this life. Who gives the fruits of these karmas? God? No. It is given by nature, or what is called 'Scientific Circumstantial Evidences' (*Vyavasthit Shakti),* by Param Pujya Shree Dadashri. It is due to ignorance that, while experiencing the karmas, *raag-dwesh* (likes-dislikes) is created, which in turn creates new seeds of karma that mature in the next life and have to be suffered. Gnanis prevent one from creating new seeds of karmas. When all karmas have been completely exhausted one attains the final *Moksha*.

When someone insults you or causes damage to you, it is all due to Scientific Circumstantial Evidences. The person is not at fault, he is only an instrument (apparent doer). How can the action originate without any cause? He (victim) himself has accumulated the cause karmas of receiving insults (from his past life), which results as an effect and manifests into physical form when all circumstances come together. Only the seeds cannot come into fruition, but all the circumstantial evidences have to be met, so the tree can grow and one can try its fruit. Until all the evidences are met, how can the fruit be achieved? We sowed the seeds of insult, but for the maturation of the fruit, all the evidences have to be met. Human beings bind karmas because of ignorance; they perceive the 'instrument' to be the doer, blaming the instrument. If one stays in Gnan then he will see that the person is only a *nimit* and therefore faultless. He will understand, "This insult is the result of my own karmas." In this way, one does not create new karmas and becomes free. If he should perceive the person to be the culprit, then he must do *pratikraman* at that very moment; "shoot on sight" so the seeds will not come into fruition in the future.

The process of the coming together of all the evidences, ripening, and experiencing the fruits of karmas is Scientific Circumstantial Evidence. Param Pujya Dadashri says that *"Vyavasthit Shakti"* (Scientific Circumstantial Evidences) is responsible for giving the fruit.

Atmavignani Purush Param Pujya Shree Dada Bhagwan has imparted this "science of karma" to the world. We have presented it here in an abridged book version in the form of Dadavani for the readers to help them solve the confusing problems of life!

- Dr. Niruben Amin

Contents

The Science of Karma

Does One Act According To One's Free Will Or Does It Just Happen?

Dadashri: Do you ever find that you are forced to do something against your wishes? Does that happen or not?

Questioner: Yes, that does happen.

Dadashri: What is the reason for that? You do not wish to, yet you have no choice. It is the effect of karmas created in your past life.

People believe this effect to be the cause. They do not understand the previous life's effect at all. If anything done in this life were a cause, then why would you do something against your will? Furthermore, why would you say, "I did it," when you did not want to do it in the first place? Why do others say you did it, also? People call all visible actions to be the same as doing the karma. They will say, "I did a good deed today and so I created a good karma today." Whereas the Gnani Purush knows that all the visible acts of this life are an effect.

Who Sent You To This Earth?

Questioner: Are we born of our own free will or are we sent here?

Dadashri: No one sends you here. It is your karma that takes you to a place where your rebirth is to take place. If your karmas are good, you will be born in a good place and if they are bad, you will be born in a bad place.

What Is The Principle Of Karma?

Questioner: What is the definition of 'karma'?

Dadashri: Supporting any action, with the claim, "I am doing it," is karma. Claiming doership of any action, binds karma. To support the action with the belief 'I am the doer' is called binding the karma. It is this support of the belief of 'doership' that binds karma. If you know that you are not the doer and are aware of who the true doer is, 'I am not the doer' and 'who is the doer' then the action will not have any support and the karma will be shed.

Questioner: What is the principle of karma?

Dadashri: If you yell, "You are a thief!" into a well, what happens?

Questioner: You will hear the word's echo.

Dadashri: Exactly! If you don't like to hear what comes to you, then you should say, "You are a king!" instead, so that you will hear, "You are a king." Say that, which you would like to hear. Give what you would want to receive. That is the principle of karma. Karma means action. What is reaction? That is the echo. All reactions are like 'echoes' of your previous actions; the fruits will be inevitable.

What does the well illustrate here? It tells you that the world is your own projection. What you were referring to as karma, is really a projection.

Questioner: Is there a principal of karma or not?

Dadashri: The whole world is nothing but the principle of karma. The existence of bondage lies entirely on you, you are responsible for it. Everything is your own projection. You are responsible even for the formation of your body. Everything you encounter is your own design; nobody else is responsible for it. For endless lives, you have been responsible, "wholly and solely."

Your Own Projection

People recognize that whatever they experience is their own projection. As a result they try to change that projection, but are not successful. This is because the projection is not solely in their hands. Talks about changing the projection are correct, but does one have the independent ability to do so? Yes, he does, however only to a limited extent. The major portion of this control is not in your hands. Only after attaining the true knowledge does one become independent, but until then, it is not quite so.

Now how can the 'project' be stopped? (The project has components of cause and effect). Until one finds his real Self in all this, he continues to wander aimlessly. Although he recognizes, "This body and I are not one and the same". There are many other inner components within and one continues to identify with them, causing the belief of, "I am Chandubhai," to remain. It is due to his inability to break free of this belief, that man thinks he is the 'doer'. He believes that he is the one that speaks, that he is the one doing the penance, and *samayik* etc. As long as he believes he is the doer, he continues to create new projects and suffer the consequences of the old (past life causes) ones. If people understood the principles of karma, they would understand the principle of liberation.

Bondage Through Wrong Belief

Dadashri: What is your name?

Questioner: Chandubhai.

Dadashri: Are you really Chandubhai?

Questioner: What else can I say? It is what everyone thinks is correct.

Dadashri: Then you really are Chandubhai, are you not? Are you not sure of that? You say, "My name is Chandubhai."

Questioner: I am sure.

Dadashri: You say, "My name is Chandubhai," not "I am Chandubhai." Then are you really Chandubhai, or are you something else?

Questioner: That is true that we are something different. That is a known fact.

Dadashri: No. 'Chandubhai' is a means to identify this body. You know that 'Chandubhai' is the name of this body, but who are *you*? Should you not know that?

Questioner: Yes, indeed I ought to. I should make an effort to find out.

Dadashri: So in essence what you are doing, is taking advantage of everything in 'Chandubhai's' name. You claim to be Chandubhai when all along you are not. Under the name of Chandubhai, you are enjoying all the pleasures: "I am this lady's husband," "I am his uncle," etc... and consequently, binding endless karmas, through these false beliefs.

As long as you are influenced by this false imposition, you are binding karmas. When, the question "Who am I?" is resolved, you will no longer bind karmas.

At the present time you are binding karma, even in your sleep, because you go to sleep believing that you are Chandubhai. The Lord says that the biggest karma of all is to shove the Self into a sack before sleeping, with the belief, "I am Chandulal."

Doership Binds Karma

Questioner: How is karma bound? Would you please explain that further?

Dadashri: I will explain to you how karma is bound.

You remain bound when you are not doing any karma and yet you believe that you are doing it. Not even God is the doer. If he were, then he too would be bound by karmas. Neither you nor God is the doer.

When you pass your exams, you say, "I passed!" yet, there is another force that prevails behind your success. To believe, "I did it!" is the false imposition, and that is why you bind karma.

Even Vedanta Accepts God As The Non-doer

Questioner: So if things happen because of some other power, then it would not matter whether one steals or gives to charity.

Dadashri: Yes, you can say that both are the same, but people do not keep them as such. Those that give to charity bind karma because they walk around with inflated egos. The thief too, binds karma when he says, "No one will ever catch me!" Nothing will touch you, as long as you do not hold the belief, "I did it".

Questioner: In the initial stage there is a belief that God is the doer. Going further, the *Vedas* maintain that God is not the doer. The *Upanishads* say the same. God is not the doer; everyone has to suffer the fruits of his own karmas. Do the consequences of karma continue life after life?

Dadashri: Yes of course! Karma is like the fruit of a mango tree. The mango will yield the tree and the tree will yield the mango and the cycle continues.

Questioner: That is the principle of Evolution. It keeps continuing.

Dadashri: No. That is the effect of karma. The mango is the fruit, which will have the seed that will grow into the tree, which in turn will yield the fruit. This will continue on. Karma disperses the seeds of karma on and on…

Questioner: Therefore people will then continue creating good and bad karmas and never be free.

Dadashri: Yes, the pulp of the mango is eaten and the stone seed is thrown out.

Questioner: And on that site will sprout a new mango tree.

Dadashri: There is no escape.

If you believe that God is the doer, then why do you also believe that you are the 'doer'? Then you too become a doer. Humans are the only species that believe 'I am the doer'. Whenever one becomes a doer, there is a breakdown in dependency on God. God says, "Since you are the 'doer', then you and I are both free! Do what you want." Then what use do you have for God?

When one believes that he is the 'doer', he binds karma. When one ceases to believe that he is the 'doer', his karma effects will come to an end.

The Essence Of All Scriptures

That is why Akha Bhagat (Famous Saint) spoke these words,

If you are Jiva (mortal), the doer is Hari (God).
If you are Shiva, (Shuddhatma-pure Soul) that is the truth.

It means that if you are a pure Soul, then you are correct. And if you are a mortal living being, then the one above, God, is the doer. The truth is that you are a pure Soul and that there is no one up there by the name of God who is your superior. So when the difference between *Jiva* and *Shiva* is gone, one is ready to become the *Parmatma* (the Supreme Soul). When people pray to God they are separating themselves from the Lord. Here, after receiving Gnan (the knowledge of Self-realization), the *Jiva-Shiva* difference is gone and the separation is eliminated.

The second verse of the poem reads:

When you relinquish the doership, you are free of karma. That is the secret meaning of this great verse.

Charging of karmas occurs with the incorrect belief of, "I am Chandubhai and I did this." After receiving Atma Gnan (the knowledge that you are the pure Soul), you are no longer Chandubhai. In the world's day-to-day interactions you are Chandubhai, but in reality, you are not. In reality you are the Self. "I did this," is a phrase that is applicable only to your daily interactions. The cycle of karma is broken once your sense of doership goes. After acquiring the Self, Chandubhai, is the doer, you are not.

When the awareness of, "I am not the doer," is firmly established in your conviction, new karmas will stop binding and new causes (karma) will not be created. The old karmas will discharge. This is the meaning of the great spiritual verse. It is the essence of all the scriptures.

The Doer Is The Sufferer

Questioner: Our scriptures say that everyone reaps the fruit of karma depending upon their deeds.

Dadashri: Each person is responsible for himself. God has never interfered in this. There is no one above us. You are independent in this world. All along you have been accustomed to being subordinate and that is why you have a 'boss' over you. Otherwise there is no one above you, nor is there a subordinate. That is how the world is. This simply needs to be understood.

I have roamed the entire universe and have not found a single place where an almighty power exists. There is no such Almighty who goes by the name of God. There is no so-called God above you. You are responsible for yourself. People everywhere believe that God created this world. Those who believe in the principle of reincarnation cannot believe that God created the world. What is reincarnation based on? It is based on the concept, "I am the doer and I am the sufferer. I am reaping the fruits of my own karma. God does not interfere in this!"

Questioner: Up until now, I used to think that God was responsible for all this.

Dadashri: No. The responsibility is your own. You are wholly and solely responsible. When a person gets shot, he is suffering the effect of his past life's karma. The person who does the shooting will suffer when his karma is ready to give fruits.

It is just like a mango. You will not be able to extract any juice out of the mango the day you buy it. You can only do that when it ripens. Similarly, the time has to be just right for the person to receive the bullet. The fact that the bullet is received means that the fruit has ripened and the juice has come out. The one who shot the bullet, his fruit is now small and is growing and will ripen in time. Thereafter the juice will come out (the result of karma).

Who Is Bound: Body Or Soul?

Questioner: Now, is it the body or the soul that is bound?

Dadashri: The body itself is karma, so how can it have any other bondage? He, who feels that he is not free, is bound. Who suffers imprisonment, the prison or the prisoner? So this body is the prison, and the one within, is bound. The one who believes, "I am bound, I am this body, I am Chandubhai," is the one who is bound.

Questioner: Do you mean to say that the soul binds (charges) and discharges karma through the body?

Dadashri: No, it is not like that. The soul is absolutely not involved in this. In fact the soul is free; it is independent. It is the ego, which has been created through false impositions that binds karma, and it is the ego that experiences the fruits of karma. You are the pure Self and yet you claim that you are Chandubhai. Claiming to something you are not, is called the ego. This is the false imposition of the ego. Egoism is to usurp someone else's space and call it your own. When this ego leaves, you can return to your own place, where there is no bondage.

Karma And Soul: Together Life After Life

Questioner: So is it possible for the soul to be free from karma? When does that happen?

Dadashri: When no circumstance can cling and attach to the Self, then not a single karma will cling or attach to him. No karmas exist for the Absolute liberated Souls and such are only to be found in the *Siddhagati* (domain of the liberated souls).

One is subject to karma bondage only in the universe of life; and this has been the case for time immemorial. Furthermore, it is all scientific circumstantial evidence. All this has come about as a result of the constant motion of elements. This gives rise to illusion, which in turn gives rise to the ego in man.

Illusion itself is the identification with that which is not real, the non-Self. Amidst all this illusion the Self is forgotten. So there has never been a time that the soul has been free of karma.

By the time one meets a Gnani Purush, a considerable weight of karma has been shed. In fact it is when his karmas become lighter that he is able to meet a Gnani Purush. The meeting of the two is also scientific, it happens when all the scientific circumstantial evidences come together. Such a meeting cannot occur through one's own efforts. This meeting simply happens and one's work gets accomplished.

Karma is the coming together of circumstances, and its nature is dissipation (to discharge).

The Relationship Of Karma And Soul

Questioner: What is the relationship between the soul and karma?

Dadashri: Both will separate if the link of doership between the two is broken. Each will go to its own place.

Questioner: I did not understand that very well.

Dadashri: Without doership there is no karma. With doership there is karma. If you are not the doer, then no matter what you do, you will not bind any karma.

Questioner: Then is karma the doer?

Dadashri: The doer is the doer. Karma is not the doer. Do you say, "I did it," or do you say, "Karma did it?"

Questioner: The internal belief that "I am doing it," is always there. We always say, "I did it!"

Dadashri: Yes, you say, "I am doing it," and hence you become the doer. In reality neither the karma nor the soul is the doer.

Questioner: The soul is on one side and karma is on the other. How can the two be separated?

Dadashri: They are separate. They seem to be connected because of this link of doership. Once this doership goes, the one who claims to be the doer also disappears, and the two will be separate.

Karma Is Bound Through Internal Actions

Questioner: Does karma apply to human beings?

Dadashri: Human beings do nothing but bind karma, constantly. The human ego is such that even though it does not eat, drink, or conduct any actions in the worldly life, it still maintains a notion of doership, which is why it binds karma. Karma is bound through the ego that says, "I am doing it." Is it not a wonder that happens? It can be proven that the ego does not eat, drink, or do anything else. It can also be proven that in spite of not doing anything, it binds karmas. Only humans bind karmas.

Questioner: Because of the body, one has to eat and drink, but despite this, is it possible that one is not the doer of karma?

Dadashri: One cannot see karma being bound. People generally think of karma as something that is visible to the eye. They may see someone hurt another person and assume that that is how the person charges karma. Is that not what people believe?

Questioner: Yes, they say it as they see it.

Dadashri: People believe that karma is the external activities people do, such as eating, sleeping, hitting someone, etc. People label all actions as 'karma'. But in reality the activity they see is really the fruit of karma, not the actual karma itself.

Whenever karma is bound, there is internal suffering. What does a child do when you give him bitter medicine? He makes a face! And when you give him medicine that is sweet, he will like it. When people do *raag-dwesh* (attachment-abhorrence) they are planting causes that give rise to new karma. You will have to experience karma that you like and also the ones you dislike. The ones you do not like will leave you hurting while those you like will leave you happy. The causes that were created in your past life bring fruits to you, in this life.

Laws Governing The Sowing Of The Seeds Of Karma

Questioner: Is there any way of knowing which seed will flourish and which will not?

Dadashri: Yes, for example when you say, "The snack

was delicious and I ate it all," you are sowing the seed. There is nothing wrong in saying, "I ate," as long as you are aware that you are not the one who is eating. But instead you become the doer and when you take on the doership, you plant the seed of karma.

When you have no abhorrence towards the one who curses you, and no attachment towards the one who garlands you and takes care of you, then karma will not bind. *Raag* is attachment. *Dwesh* is abhorrence.

Questioner: What if we do not realize that *raag* and *dwesh* are occurring?

Dadashri: The reward for not knowing is the wandering into life after life.

The Relationship Of The Self And Body

Questioner: Can you explain the relationship between the body and the Self in more detail?

Dadashri: The body has come about as a result of ignorance of the Self. It is the effect of all the causes you created. When someone praises you, you are pleased, but when he insults you, it upsets you. The external display of emotion is immaterial. The internal intent of these reactions (attachment and abhorrence) is the cause. It is this inner reaction that will bind karma. And it is this karma that will be discharged in the next life as an effect. The mind, speech and body, are all effective. While experiencing the effects, one creates new causes. The cycle of cause and effect is perpetuated in this manner. Even the foreign scientists can understand the concept of reincarnation in this way!

These are all effects. To plead a case in a court of law is also an effect. You must not have any ego during this effect by saying, "I won the case." Effects will follow naturally, like flowing water. The water does not say, "I am going down."

Even then it travels a great distance to the ocean. Humans on the other hand, have ego and so they bind karma. If a lawyer wins a lawsuit he will say, "I won the lawsuit." Claiming doership is the ego, and this binds karma; the ego creates a cause. In return, the fruit of this cause will come as an effect.

The Mystery Of Cause And Effect

Do you understand effect now? That which is happening is effect. When you submitted your examination paper (past life), it was the cause. You do not have to worry about the effect, the result, which is inevitable once the exam is given. The result is the effect. The whole world is preoccupied with the effect, and strives to change it, when really it should be concerned about the cause.

Do you understand this science? Science is based on principles. It is irrefutable. If you were to earn two million in your business, would that be a cause or an effect?

Questioner: It is a cause.

Dadashri: Explain to me how it can be a cause. Does it happen according to your will?

Questioner: When you do business, whatever is going to happen will happen. That would be effect. But one has to create the causes in order to do the business, doesn't he? Only then will he be able to do the business, right?

Dadashri: No. Cause means nothing of the outside world is necessary. You can only do the business if your health is good; you have a sound mind and you have the necessary capital. That which is dependent upon all these things is an effect. But when a man stays up worrying at night, he is creating a cause; there is nothing else necessary in that. Causes are independent.

Questioner: Is the business we conduct an effect, then?

Dadashri: I call it an effect. Business is an effect. Do you have to do anything with the result of an exam? You have to do something when you take the exam, which is considered a cause. But do you have to do anything for the result?

Questioner: No.

Dadashri: Similarly even here, you do not have to do anything. Everything happens on its own accord. Your body is used in the process and things just happen. For causes, however, one has to do something. The belief of doership, 'I did it', is the cause. The suffering of that effect, 'I am suffering', is also the cause. Everything else is effect.

Questioner: All the inner intents are causes.

Dadashri: Yes, cause requires no one's help. When you cook a wonderful meal, it is all an effect, but if in the process, you internally feel (inner intent) "I am a great cook. I made a wonderful meal," it is this intent that is the cause. As long as you do not have this inner intent, it is all effect. All that you hear or see is effect. Causes cannot be seen.

Questioner: So effect is everything that one experiences through these five senses?

Dadashri: Yes. All that is an effect. Your whole life is an effect. *Bhaav* is the inner intent in life. This is the cause. There is a doer of this *bhaav*. It is called the 'ego' ("I am Chandulal, and this is happening to me, I am suffering."). Whatever *bhaavs* (inner intent) occur in your life, if you are the 'doer' of those *bhaavs*, then they are all considered 'causes'. That is what everyone in this world does.

Once the karma ceases to bind, that is the end. Are you able to understand this much? Do you think that you can stop binding karma? Have you ever seen that happen? When you become involved in good things, you bind good karma. The bad things are always there. You can never get rid of karma. Once you become aware of who you are and what makes all this happen, you will stop binding karma, forever.

How Did The First Karma Arise?

Questioner: According to the theory of karma, one binds karma and then suffers its consequence later. So in a sense, it is cause and effect: First comes the cause, then comes its effect. So according to your inference, how can you trace back to the original karma?

Dadashri: There is no beginning in that which has no beginning. It is like a beaded necklace. Where is the beginning of the earth's rotation and orbit?

Questioner: It has no beginning.

Dadashri: Therefore there is no beginning for this world. It is all round. It has no beginning. But there is liberation from this. Liberation is possible due to the presence of the Self. Everything is round, not square. If it were square, it could be said that it starts from one corner and ends at another. Where is there a corner in something round? The entire universe is round, but your intellect cannot perceive this. So tell your intellect to stand aside. The intellect cannot fathom this, but it can be understood through Gnan.

Which comes first, the egg or the chicken? Alas, just leave it alone and talk about something else, or else you will be doomed to the cycle of birth and death like the chickens and the egg. Anything that has no solution is round. Don't you hear of people talking in circles?

Questioner: Still the question keeps arising about where the original karma comes from before birth. In the cycle of eight million and four hundred thousand births and deaths, when and where did all this *paap* (demerit karma) and *punya* (merit karma) begin?

Dadashri: It has no beginning.

Questioner: It has to have a beginning somewhere.

Dadashri: It started when the intellect began and it will end when the intellect ends. Otherwise it has no beginning.

Questioner: Who gave us this intellect?

Dadashri: Where is there a giver in all this anyway? There is nobody above you. If someone were to be your giver, then he would be your superior and he would always remain as such. There would be no such thing as liberation in the world. How can there be liberation when you have a superior?

Questioner: But what was the first karma? What was the original karma that gave rise to this body?

Dadashri: Nobody has given you this body. It is all a result of the coming together and interactions of the six eternal elements. In reality, you have not been given this body. You have assumed this body to be yours. This is your illusion. When this illusion goes away, there will be nothing there. It all came about because of the belief, "I am Chandubhai."

Karma Of One Or Numerous Lives?

Questioner: All these karmas cannot give effect in just one lifetime. So does that mean that one has to suffer them over a period of many lifetimes? How can one attain liberation unless all his karmas are finished?

Dadashri: One cannot even begin to think about liberation. When the karmas for a particular lifetime come to end, that is when the body departs. But by then new karmas have already been bound. So, how can one talk about liberation? Old karmas (effects), from the previous life, do not follow you. You are binding karmas even at this very moment. While you are engaged here, asking these questions, you are binding *punya* karmas (good karma).

Who Is The Doer, And Who Is The Sufferer?

Questioner: Dada. We have to suffer the consequences of karmas from our past life, in our current life. But the karmas that the body in our previous life suffered would have been extinguished with that body in the funeral pyre. When the soul is completely pure (*nirvikaar*) and takes on a new body, why does the new body have to endure the karma of the previous body?

Dadashri: The previous body suffered the consequences of its own karma.

Questioner: So?

Dadashri: These karmas were created in the mind. They are subtle karmas. These karmas are the causes, which create the causal body.

Questioner: That is all fine, but did that body not have *bhaavs* (inner intent)?

Dadashri: It is not the body that does the *bhaavs*.

Questioner: Then?

Dadashri: The physical body has suffered the fruits of its action. It experienced suffering when it received two slaps, but that which has already been in the planning, is coming into visible action now. The slaps received is an effect. The cause for this effect was planned in the past life.

Questioner: Yes, but who did the planning? Was it not the previous body that did the planning?

Dadashri: The body has nothing to do with it. It is all the doing of the ego.

Of This Life: In This Life?

Questioner: Do we suffer the consequences of all these karmas in just this lifetime or will we have to suffer them in the next lifetime as well?

Dadashri: The karmas from the previous life were in the form of a plan, as though designed on a piece of paper. Now when it materializes and comes into fruition, it is called *prarabdha* (fate). It may take so many years for it to mature, perhaps fifty, seventy-five, even a hundred years.

So karmas that were bound in the previous life, may take numerous years before they come into fruition. People generally think that karmas are being bound when they are actually in the process of coming into fruition or discharging.

If you slap someone, people would say that you have bound karma. If you were to ask them what karma you bound, they will tell you that it was the karma from the act of slapping. Now, there is no doubt that the person you slapped is going to react. He may not react straight away, but later on when he gets the chance, he will take his revenge. People will then say you finally received payment of your karma for slapping him. That is called suffering the consequences here and now. But you have to agree with what they say and tell them that they are correct, even though they will not be able to tell you the reason behind why the other person received the slap. They will not be able to find the reason either. They will insist that you are the one who did it, whereas it is the fruition of one's karma that makes a person do things. It is the effect of previously created causes that makes you 'do' things.

Questioner: So the slap is the fruit of karma (effect), and not the cause of karma itself, true?

Dadashri: Yes, it is the fruit of karma. It is your unfolding karma that makes you slap him. What if the person you slapped requests you to slap him again? You will not do it. There was a reason for the first slap. You both had a pending karmic account with one another, which ends there. Nothing happens outside the realm of both your accounts. There is no need to be afraid in the world. Do not lose sleep over it, but guard yourself against the arrogance of the belief that nothing will happen to you.

Karma Effects: Worldly View, And Gnani's View

Questioner: It is said that whatever has to be suffered, has to be suffered here in this life. What is wrong with that?

Dadashri: Yes, but that is what the world believes. What is the reality in this?

If a person binds karma of pride through ego in his previous life, then in this life when all the buildings are being constructed, he will become unduly proud and say, "Look at my buildings, they are better than the others." Why does he become so proud? It is because of his pride-karma. People believe that he is binding karma through his proud and arrogant behavior. They call this karma. Really it is the fruit or effect of his past karma. 'Fruit' means that he is forced to become arrogant against his will; it just happens, and is visible to the world.

What the world labels as arrogance, anger, egoistic etc., their results are suffered in this very life. A person pays for his negative qualities in this lifetime when people say that he is conceited, ill tempered and arrogant. He suffers the effects of his egoistic arrogance when people call him conceited and discredit his reputation. The consequences of his arrogance and egoistic behavior are that in this very lifetime, he will be disgraced or discredited. But if in his arrogance he feels from within that his actions are wrong and that he needs to get rid of his weaknesses, he is then binding a new karma of humility for his next life. Because of this new *bhaav*, he will be humble in his next life.

This is the theory of karma. If your *bhaav* changes while you are doing something wrong, then you will bind a new karma, based on your new *bhaav*. But if you rejoice over doing something wrong, then you will bind a new and stronger karma, the consequences of which you will have to suffer.

It is worth understanding this whole science. This science of the *Vitarags* is very mysterious.

In This Life Or The Next?

Questioner: Will one experience the consequences of karmas created in this life, in the next life?

Dadashri: Yes, he will not experience them in this life.

Questioner: So what we are experiencing now, is the result of our previous life?

Dadashri: Yes, it is from the past life. But simultaneously you are binding new karmas for the next life. That is why your new karmas should be good. This life is decided, but make sure you do the right thing for the next one.

Questioner: People are not able to do good karmas because of the effect and power of this current time cycle called 'Kaliyug.'

Dadashri: There is no need for good karma.

Questioner: So what is needed then?

Dadashri: There is a need for good *bhaavs* (intentions) within. Good karmas can only be done if one's *prarabdha* (fate) is good. But good intentions (*bhaavs*) can be made, even without good *prarabdha*.

When Does Bad Karma Give Results?

Questioner: How can one be liberated when he has to experience the consequences of good and bad karmas in this or the next life?

Dadashri: The consequences of karma is not the problem, it is the seeds of karma that are destructive. On the path to liberation, if one ceases to sow new seeds, the fruits of past karmas will come and leave. The soul is then liberated. Once new karmas are created, you will have to experience their consequences. They will not let you go and that is why they are obstructive. With past consequences, you merely have to taste the fruits and move on.

Questioner: You said that one would have to experience even the smallest of karmas, if created.

Dadashri: Yes, you have no choice but to suffer them. There is no way out. You can be liberated even while experiencing the fruits of past karma, but liberation is impossible if one continues to bind new karmas, because he will have to stay back to reap the consequences of the karma.

Questioner: Do we experience the fruits of our good and bad karma in this lifetime or in the next?

Dadashri: The consequences of karmas that are visible, for example when a person steals, cheats, and betrays others, are suffered in this life. While suffering them the internal intent of attachment and abhorrence is the seed for new karmas, which will have to be suffered in the next life.

Every Life: A Balance Sheet Of Previous Lives

Questioner: Are the karmas today in my life, an accumulation from countless past lives?

Dadashri: Every life is the balance of infinite previous lives. It is a balance sheet. This applies to all past lives. It is not a total sum of all lives. According to the law of nature, when the time is right the karma must come into fruition, otherwise a lot of karmas will be left over.

Questioner: Is this all linked to the past life?

Dadashri: Yes. One cannot do both; create cause and suffer its effect, in one lifetime. Why can one not create both at the same time? How can cause and effect have the same time period? First a fulfillment of a certain time period is required before a cause becomes an effect. Nothing will happen without this time period. It is like a mango tree. First the tree will produce blossoms and then the mango. Is time not intrinsic in the process of maturation? Does it ripen in just one day? Similarly some of the karmas that one binds need a hundred years to ripen before they give fruit.

Questioner: So are the karmas of this life the result of karmas caused in the last life or are they also the causes from many other lives prior to that?

Dadashri: No, nature is not like that. Nature is very precise and meticulous. For example, the balance sheet of karma (merit and demerit) created in your ten lifetimes ago, was carried forward in the life nine lifetimes ago. The balance sheet of the life nine lifetimes ago was carried forward in the life eight lifetimes ago and so on. The balance sheet does not carry forward all the karmas; only the balance is carried forward. Whatever the longevity of the person, he will bring with him karmas of that time duration; but the karmas are of only one lifetime. You cannot say that they are of two lifetimes.

Karma requires time to come into fruition; for some people it may take five hundred to even a thousand years to mature. Nevertheless in the balance sheet it is still new.

Questioner: They are carried forward.

Dadashri: Yes, the old account goes into the new account. Nothing is left behind. They are bound in the form of causes and to take effect, it may take anywhere between fifty to seventy-five years.

Who Controls All This?

Questioner: So who manages all this?

Dadashri: The rules of karma are such that when you

create karma, the result will come naturally and automatically.

Questioner: Who decides the fruits of karmas we have to experience? Who makes us experience these?

Dadashri: They do not need to be decided. The karma itself does this. It happens on its own.

Questioner: Then who governs the rules of karma?

Dadashri: When two atoms of Hydrogen and one of Oxygen come together, we automatically get water. That is the rule of karma.

Questioner: But somebody must have made that rule?

Dadashri: Nobody makes the rules; otherwise there would be a creator. Nobody has to make the rules. This puzzle has come about on its own governed by the laws of science. I am telling you that this world is run only by Scientific Circumstantial Evidences. In Gujarati I call it '*Vyavasthit Shakti*'.

Vyavasthit Shakti And Karma

Questioner: Is what you call '*Vyavasthit*' according to karma?

Dadashri: The world is not run by karmas, *Vyavasthit* runs it. Who brought you here to *satsang*? Was it your karma? No, *Vyavasthit* brought you here. Karma is there all the same, so why did it not bring you here yesterday. Why did it bring you here today? *Vyavasthit* brings together the time, inner intent, space etc. All these circumstances come together to bring you here. Karma is only a small part of *Vyavasthit*. When the circumstances are right, one claims, "I did it," but what happens when the circumstances are not right?

The Fruit Comes Automatically

Questioner: If someone else brings the karma-fruit (fruit of karma), is it still another karma?

Dadashri: No one else can give the fruit of karma. No such person has yet been born. If you were to drink poison, you would die. No one is needed in the middle to bring the results.

If someone were needed to deliver karma-fruits, then he would have to have a gigantic office. Everything runs scientifically. There is no need for a middleman. When the time is up for maturation of karma, it automatically comes into effect. Just like these mangoes that ripen automatically.

Questioner: Yes.

Dadashri: They ripen on the tree, do they not? These karmas are like mangoes that ripen on the tree. When the time is right, they ripen and are ready for consumption.

Questioner: If the karma one creates in this life gives result in the next life, who keeps the account of all that?

Dadashri: Why does the water inside a pipe freeze in winter? It is because the environment has turned cold. It is all Scientific Circumstantial Evidence. All these karmas yielding their fruit are evidences. Who makes you hungry? It is all Scientific Circumstantial Evidences.

The Order Behind The Effect Of Karma

Questioner: In which order do the effects of karmas come? Is it in the same order as they were bound?

Dadashri: No, it is not like that.

Questioner: Can you explain how it is?

Dadashri: They are all arranged according to their inherent properties, for example the ones to be experienced during the day, during the night, during times of happiness and during bad times. This is how they are arranged.

Questioner: What is this arrangement based on?

Dadashri: According to the inherent nature of the karma. We all gather in a group because of the compatibility of our natural characteristics.

Seen Through Absolute Knowledge

Questioner: How can one tell whether karma is old (effect) or new (cause)?

Dadashri: Nobody can see karmas being created. Only the One with Absolute Knowledge knows it. There is not even a trace of new karma in the karma you witness in the world. New karmas are not created as long as one remains the Knower and Observer of the karma that is unfolding. But if one becomes involved ("I am the doer, I am the sufferer."), then he will bind new karma. It is only after you attain Self-realization, that you cease to bind new karmas.

One cannot see the Self or charge karmas in the world. Only the effect of karma is visible. When people taste and become engrossed in the fruit of karma, they become the doers or sufferers of the karma.

Why At This Time?

Questioner: Many times I feel that we are binding bad karmas, whilst externally the karma unfolding is an auspicious one.

Dadashri: Yes. That can happen. The karma unfolding presently may be auspicious but from within one is binding *paap* (demerit) karma.

Let me give you an example. You and four of your friends have traveled to this city from a village but cannot find accommodation anywhere because you arrive very late. You tell your friends that you have a friend that lives in the city and that he may be able to put all of you up for the night. You arrive at this friend's house at around 11:30 pm and you knock on the door. Your friend first sees only you and then realizes that you are not alone, but there are five of you. Is he likely to tell you to go back when he sees the five of you? Of course, he will not. Instead he is courteous and invites you all inside. Our people are generally very polite.

Questioner: Yes, he will invite us all in.

Dadashri: Your friend would welcome you and make you comfortable, but what do you think he is thinking in his mind? He is thinking, "What on earth are they doing here this late in the night?" That inner *bhaav* is what binds karma. There is no need for him to do that, the visitors have come to him because of a pending karmic account, and they will stay as long as the account remains. Once the account is over, they will leave. But through his internal *bhaav* he has created a new karma.

Now if he were to ask me what he should do for his spoiled *bhaav*, I would tell him to ask for forgiveness from whichever God he believed in. If you ask for forgiveness and vow not to repeat the mistake again, that new karma (cause) will be erased immediately. Changes in a letter that has been written are possible provided that you have not yet mailed it. Once the letter is mailed (you have left this life), it is no longer in your hands and the karma has been bound (caused). You can erase everything before you leave this body.

Your friend, in this case has already bound that karma. He asks you if you would like some tea or coffee and you tell him that you would rather have some hot food instead. His wife, who is in bed, overhears this and gets upset. Alas! more karmas are being bound! At that time, it is the law of nature that is in operation. Visitors come because of a pending account, so one should not spoil his *bhaav*. He should stay within the laws of nature and offer the visitors whatever he can. Even the leftovers from the evening meal would be adequate. The visitors are not demanding anything elaborate. Instead what people do is try to make a good impression by making an elaborate meal, while all along in their minds they are cursing the visitors for the inconvenience. That is called karma. It should not be this way.

Therefore Never Spoil Your Inner Intent

Questioner: How are good and bad karmas bound?

Dadashri: The intention of giving happiness to others binds good karma and the intention of hurting others, will bind bad karmas. It is only through intent and not through action that karmas are bound. The external actions may be good or bad. That does not bind karma. What causes bondage of karmas is the inner intent. Therefore be aware of the inner intent and do not spoil it. The external acts are all effects.

If the motive behind an action is selfish, it will bind demerit karma. Demerit karmas bring unhappiness. If there is no selfish intent then you will bind merit karma. Merit karmas bring happiness. But nevertheless, both are karmas. The shackle of good karma is made of gold and the shackle of bad karmas is made of iron. Both prevent liberation. Both are shackles.

Visible Karma-Effect: Subtle Karma-Cause

A wealthy businessman donates fifty thousand rupees to a charity. His friend asks him why he did so and the businessman tells him that he would not have donated a single penny had it not been for the pressure from the mayor. Now what will be the fruit of this? The donation he made is the visible karma, the rewards of which he will get in this life when people praise and admire him for his generosity. But even while people praise him for his generosity, what is he charging within? The consequence of *bhaav* karma of, "I would not give even a single penny...," he will experience in his next life. In his next life he will not be able to donate even a single penny! This is the subtle karma, which is the cause for the next life's effect. The donation made in this life was an effect. Now who can understand something so subtle?

On the other hand a poor man is asked to make a contribution for the same charity, and his response is that he has only five rupees with him, which they can have. He further tells them that he would donate five *lakh* rupees without any hesitation if he had that kind of money. He is sincere about this. His donation of five rupees is the discharge of karma created in his past life, but what does he charge subtly? A karma where in his next life he will be able to donate five *lakh* rupees when this karma comes into fruition.

A person may appear to be a generous donor on the outside, making a lot of donations to religious causes, and may appear to be very active in religious activities, while on the inside he may be scheming to take money which does not rightfully belong to him.

This person's visible action is an effect and for it he will receive praise here in this life. He has created a new life of misery for himself for the causes, which exist within him. Donations, charitable deeds etc., are all visible karma, the benefits of which are reaped in this life. People believe that these visible karmas are the charge karma for the next life. In fact, it is the subtle karma, happening within, that are charge karma and these will come into fruition in the next life.

If a person were to steal today, his action of stealing would be the visible karma. The fruit of this karma will be there in this lifetime; he will be disgraced and punished. All visible karmas are simply an effect and there is no cause in that which is visible. Only subtle karma, otherwise known as 'inner intent,' is of importance. The whole world however, strives to change the visible karma, by focusing on acts and behavior.

The monks and ascetics, who practice meditation and

penance etc, do so because of their effect karma. There is no cause karma in these outer acts of theirs. Their actions today is their karma effect, the fruits of which they will experience in this life when people give them credit for their penance.

Actions Do Not Charge: Intentions Do

When these religious teachers do *pratikraman, samayik,* or give lectures, their conduct is their effect karma. It is the internal charging that is important. Their conduct today is all a discharge, of charge from the past life. Their entire external conduct is in the form of discharge. When people say that they did meditation or gave alms, they will reap the rewards of these actions in their present lifetime, but of what use is this for their next life? One may be doing *samayik* externally, but only God knows what is going on internally.

A man is doing *samayik* (introspective meditation) when someone calls for him at the door. The wife answers the door. She is asked where the husband is. The wife tells his visitor, "He has gone to the trash dumping ground." The man overhears this conversation and upon introspection he finds that his wife is correct. Internally he was indeed meditating and in his meditation, he had been visiting bad places. This is the causal karma, while on the outside he is doing *samayik,* an effect karma. It would be acceptable to be doing *samayik* internally even though externally it would not be evident.

Thus Change The Inner Intent

Effect karma is when although you try to control your anger, the anger occurs. Does this happen or not?

Questioner: It happens.

Dadashri: The results of that anger will be there in this life. People may avoid you or slap you. You will be disgraced one way or another. To become angry is your effect karma, but it is your internal intent that is important. If from within you feel you had a right to be angry, this will create a new account for you to become angry again in your next life. But if your internal resolve is never to become angry, even though you do, you will not bind anything for the next life.

You will have to suffer the consequences of the overt visible effect karma of being angry, in this life, but you will not be causing anything for the next life, because you have the intent not to become angry. If, however you continue to think that you need to show your anger to people to keep them in line, then in your next life you will be an angry person. Therefore, the external action is overt effect karma, but during that time the internal intent, whatever it is, is cause karma.

If you understand just this much, there is no binding in overt karma. That is why I have put forward this science in a different light. Until now, people were brainwashed into believing that they were binding karmas because of their overt karma. This is why people have been wandering endlessly.

Living While Liberated

People believe that married people cannot attain liberation. You must understand that being married is not an obstacle to liberation, but your subtle cause karmas are. Your effect karmas do not interfere. That is why I have disclosed all this to you. Had I not made this science available to you, you would be suffering forever. You would be in a perpetual state of confusion and anxiety. The monks say that they will attain *Moksha* (liberation), yet how will they get liberation when they do not really know what they must sacrifice? They have merely renounced their visible attachments; that which can be seen or heard. For this they will reap benefits in this life. This however, is *Akram Vignan*: A new kind of science! It has made it very simple for many people to attain liberation. Is it possible to attain liberation by abandoning one's wife? How can you attain liberation if you hurt anyone?

So take care of all your responsibilities towards your wife and children and realize that it is all your effect karma. But make sure that in this effect, you hold no opinions that will lead you to charge karma for the next life. I have given you these five Agnas for that very reason. Guard yourself against being of the opinion that whatever you are experiencing or doing, is correct. No such opinion should be there. That is all that is required. The rest will happen naturally.

Guide Children In This Manner

Parents become indignant if their child does something wrong. They go around telling others that their child is a misfit or that he is a thief. Why must they do this? Why not simply forget? Whatever is done is done. Instead, why not change the child's internal *bhaav*? Parents today are not worthy of their parenthood; they are not certified to be parents and so they do not know how to go about changing their children's *bhaav*. If a child develops a habit of stealing, the parents will keep tormenting and punishing him. Needless to say, this excessive reaction, on the part of the parents, does not help. So what does the child do? He decides to ignore them and rebel even more by stealing more.

You have to change their *bhaav*. Talk to them affectionately. Hold them, hug them and make them understand with gentle words and make them see the recklessness of their actions. Ask them how they would feel if someone stole from them. Would it not hurt them if someone stole their money? Explain to them that in the same way they hurt the person they steal from. Eventually the children will heed you and come to realize that they have done wrong. Children become more stubborn and agitated if they are punished over and over again. All that is required is a change in the manner you deal with your children. The fact is that no one has understood cause karma, which is why everybody suffers.

Charge And Discharge Karma

Questioner: Is the doer of cause karma and effect karma different?

Dadashri: The doer is different in both cases. Effect karmas are discharge karmas. Just like a battery, they discharge their power all the time. Are they not being discharged even when we do not want them to?

Questioner: Yes.

Dadashri: That is how the effect karmas are discharge karmas. The new ones that are being charged inside are cause karmas. The ones that are being charged in this life will continue to discharge in the next life. The batteries that were charged in your past life are being discharged in this life. These batteries are, the battery of the mind, the battery of the speech, and the battery of the body. All three are discharging at this time, while new batteries are charging within.

When you speak, you believe, "I am speaking." But it is not so. It is the record that is playing; the 'battery' of speech is discharging. I do not speak. People however say, "Look how nicely I spoke." That is all egoism. Once this egoism goes, is there anything left? This egoism is ignorance of the Self. The doer is someone else, but you believe that you are the one who is doing it.

The cause karma that is being charged within then goes into a 'computer'. A person is one individual 'computer' and the other is a universal 'computer'. The cause karmas are first fed into the individual computer and then into the universal computer. The universal computer then takes over and does all the work. You will bind karma with the beliefs of, "I am Chandubhai," and "I am the doer." Once you realize your true identity, no new karma can be bound. This science is simple and straightforward. Otherwise not even a million efforts can make you the Absolute Self. This is an exact science.

Cause-Effect And Effect Of Effect

Questioner: Karmas that were charged in the past life come in the form of discharge in this life. What about the karmas of this life, can they discharge in this life or not?

Dadashri: No.

Questioner: When do they come?

Dadashri: Causes of this life are the effects for the next life. Causes of the last life are the effects of this life.

Questioner: But you have already said that some karmas are such, that they have to be experienced in this life.

Dadashri: That is what the people of the world perceive. If someone has dysentery, people would say it was because he frequently ate at restaurants. They would say that he had bound the karma by eating at the restaurants and that now he was suffering the effect of that karma. The Gnani would look at the reasons behind him eating in a restaurant; the reason behind how he learned to eat out; the reason behind how everything comes together. He was able to eat in the restaurant when all the circumstances came together. His eating in a restaurant was the result of a cause he made in his last life. When these causes come into effect, he will have to go to the restaurant and so he will end up going there, even if he does not want to. The person is left wondering why he does things against his wishes.

People without Gnan believe that one suffers because of what he does. They believe that karmas are bound and experienced in this very life. But they do not stop to ask why that person keeps eating in the restaurant against his wishes. The law that takes him there against his wishes is his past karmic account.

Questioner: He goes to the restaurant because of his

bhaavs from the past life and as a result has dysentery in this life. Is this all a discharge?

Dadashri: Going to restaurant and having dysentery are both discharge. The discharge is in nobody's hands. It is out of one's control.

If a person understands the theory of karma exactly, then he will be able to understand the way to liberation. What people call karma, the theory of karma, calls effect. People simply have no idea of cause karma. The theory of karma is that the 'cause' is when the karma was charged. It is not visible. All that is visible is the effect of karma. A man eats at a restaurant, as a result of the cause from his past life. Eating in the restaurant is the effect (fruit) of the karma. According to the theory of karma, the dysentery is the effect of the effect. The cause of the effect was created in the past life. Going to the restaurant is an effect. Dysentery is the effect of the effect.

He creates a new karma while enjoying the food at the restaurant, and he creates another while suffering the dysentery. So in essence he creates two new karmas, one while he is experiencing the results of past karma, and the other while experiencing the effect of effect.

Do Karmas Created Unintentionally Yield Their Effects?

Questioner: How much liability is there in karmas created intentionally and unintentionally? Can mistakes made inadvertently, be forgiven?

Dadashri: There is no one crazy enough to forgive you if you unknowingly kill someone. What would happen if your hand accidentally falls on burning charcoal?

Questioner: It would get scorched.

Dadashri: Instant effect. Whether you do it knowingly or unknowingly.

Questioner: If we have to suffer for mistakes made unintentionally, then how much do we have to suffer for the ones made knowingly?

Dadashri: If a man creates a lot of *punya* karma, these karmas are such that he will become a king, but he creates these karmas unintentionally, without any understanding of what he is doing. Then he will become a king without having any conscious knowledge of how to be one. In his next life he inherits his father's throne at the age of five, he reigns for about six years before being ousted by another king. Compare this to a man who becomes a king at the age of thirty, who also reigns for six years before being replaced. Of the two, which one is able to enjoy the fruit of his karma the most? They both ruled for six years.

Questioner: The older one.

Dadashri: Because he had knowingly bound good karmas, he enjoyed its fruits with awareness, while the child king, enjoyed the fruit of his karma without awareness. Similarly if you create good or bad karmas unintentionally, you will enjoy their fruits without awareness also. Do you understand that?

I will give you another example. Two friends are walking along and one of them accidentally steps on a cockroach and kills it while the other deliberately steps on another cockroach and crushes it to death. Now what did both the men do?

Questioner: Kill the cockroaches.

Dadashri: According to the laws of nature, they are both killers. Their crimes are the same. Both are guilty of killing, but their methods were different. What consequences will both of them face? They will face an insult and a couple of slaps on the face. The one who killed accidentally will come across someone who will insult him and slap him, but because he is born in a lower social status, he will not suffer the insult for too long, whereas the other one being born into a very prestigious family will receive the same kind of slaps and insult, but he suffers so much that he loses sleep for days. The duration of his suffering is considerably longer. So whatever you do, you must do it with the understanding that you are responsible for all your actions. "You are wholly and solely responsible. God is not responsible at all!"

The Effect Has To Be Experienced

Questioner: It is our own karma that impedes us.

Dadashri: Who else's then? No one else is responsible. It is your own karma that bothers you. If your wife who is normal and intelligent becomes insane all of a sudden, whom can we blame? She turns insane as a result of the timing for your own karma coming into fruition. So you should realize this and accept that it is your own account. You should tell yourself that you should settle your past accounts now. You have no choice but to experience them. I too have to experience effect karma, everyone has to, and even Lord Mahavir had to. The demigods used to harass Lord Mahavir. When the Lord was meditating they would throw insects and bedbugs on him.

Questioner: Was it not his effect karma that he had to suffer?

Dadashri: There was no way out. He understood that whatever the demigods were doing was after all, his own effect karma.

Which Karma Cause The Body To Suffer?

Questioner: What kinds of karma are responsible for causing diseases in a body?

Dadashri: Why does a person become deaf or dumb? In his previous life he misused his ears. If you were to misuse your eyes, you too would lose them. And if you misused your tongue, it too will go! You will lose the support of your legs if you misuse them. Therefore, you have to pay for whatever you misuse.

Why Must Innocent Children Suffer?

Questioner: We often see children that are crippled from birth. Some are killed in disasters. What sort of *paap* (bad karma) could these children have possibly done to suffer such a fate?

Dadashri: They have indeed done *paap*, for which the score has to be settled. An infant is born because of a pending account and if that infant dies, it is because of the account between him and his parent being settled.

Questioner: Was the child born in order to repay the parents for their own sins (past account)?

Dadashri: The account with the parents had already been determined. The child will render whatever happiness or unhappiness he is supposed to and then depart. When an infant dies, the parents will grieve but not as much as they would if they lost an adult son. The adult child would leave considerably more unhappiness in his wake. Is that not possible?

Questioner: It is true, that does happen.

Dadashri: That is why some are there to give misery, while others give their happiness for a long time. All these are relationships. Through your relationships you have to endure suffering or enjoy happiness. Relationships work both ways; people make each other happy or miserable. These relationships are relative.

Do Negative Cause Karmas Give Effect Only In This Life?

Questioner: If I broke up someone's marriage plans, will I have to suffer exactly the same consequences in my next life? Will the same person turn around and break up my marriage plans. Is the fruit of karma exactly the same as the karma itself? And is it to the same degree?

Dadashri: No. You will encounter the consequences of your meddling of this life, in the present life. All that is visible is effect karma. The effect and the effect of effect karma are experienced in this life.

Questioner: What if I am already married and I meddle in someone else's marital plans. How will the consequences of that action affect me?

Dadashri: No, you will not receive the very same consequences. The manner, in which you have hurt someone internally, will make its way back to you in some form or another. If you hurt someone's daughter, when you yourself do not have one, how can you suffer the same consequences? You will suffer the consequences in this very life. That which is in front of you is an effect and they have to be experienced in this life. The effect of cause karma done in this life will be experienced in your next life.

Questioner: If my *bhaav* (intent) is to cause someone a loss worth millions of dollars, does that mean I too will have to suffer the same type of loss?

Dadashri: No, not in terms of damage. You will suffer in another way, but to the same degree. Whatever unhappiness you give out, the same amount of unhappiness will come your way. Your son will make you miserable perhaps by squandering away all your money. You will inevitably suffer the same amount of unhappiness that you caused to another. If you hurt somebody, you will suffer hurt, and if you give happiness to someone, you will get happiness back. Ultimately, all the karmas fall into the category of *raag-dwesh* (attraction and abhorrence). The effect of *raag* (attraction) is happiness and the effect of *dwesh* (abhorrence) is unhappiness.

Questioner: If the effect of attraction is happiness and the effect of abhorrence, is unhappiness, would it be a direct or an indirect effect?

Dadashri: It is nothing but a direct effect. With attachment, merit karmas result and you receive prosperity and wealth. But when your wealth leaves, it will leave you with unhappiness.

The happiness that you experience is really borrowed happiness, on loan to you. Only accept it if you are going to pay it back (return to the world in another life). If you do not have the means to pay back, then stop enjoying the happiness (do not create a cause karma). It is all on loan. Every form of happiness or misery is on loan. The fruit of *punya* is happiness and that too is on loan. And the fruit of *paap* is misery, which too is on loan. Everything is on loan to you so don't make a deal if you do not want to take another birth to repay the loan. That is why both forms of karma, merit and demerit are to be renounced.

Questioner: If we are just taking back what we had previously given, the account is settled. How can you call it taking a loan?

Dadashri: Whatever happiness you are enjoying now is not something that is coming back to you. You enjoy it all the same, but you will have to make a payment for doing so. You will have to repay it. How will you repay? When you eat a mango and it is sweet, you delight in it and feel content. But the next time you eat a mango and it is sour, you will be equally unhappy. Remember if you do not take any pleasure (I am enjoying) in anything, you will not experience unhappiness (I am suffering).

Questioner: What if one does not become engrossed in it?

Dadashri: Then there is no harm in eating the mango.

Mother-in-Law: Daughter-in-Law - Both Faultless

Questioner: I have a lot of conflicts with my mother-in-law, how can I be free from them?

Dadashri: You should become free from each and every karma. Each time your mother-in-law gives you trouble, you should find freedom from that karma. What should you do for that? You should think of her as being faultless. Ask yourself why she would be at fault. Tell yourself that it is because of your own karmas that you have encountered her. She is merely instrumental in giving your effect to you. This is how you will achieve freedom from karma. On the other hand, if you look at her faults, you will increase your own karma. When you see fault in others, you bind karmas (cause) and when you look at your own faults, the karmas leave.

We should live our life in a way that does not bind any karma. You should remain detached from this world. It is because of the karmas we have bound that we encounter the people we do in this life. Who are all these people in our family? We have bound a karmic account with them, which is why they are around us. Even if you were to decide that you do not want to speak with them, you would be compelled to speak anyway. This is all a result of vengeance created in your previous life.

Questioner: That is all you see everywhere.

Dadashri: That is why I am telling you to move away from all that and come to me (The Gnani Purush and His Gnan). I will give you whatever I have experienced, so that you too will become free. There is no freedom otherwise.

I do not place blame on anyone, but I do make a note of what this world is about. I have seen the world from all aspects and in every way possible. When we see faults in others, it means that we ourselves are still at fault. At some point in time you will have to see the world as faultless. Everything around you has arisen because of your own account. It will be extremely useful to you if you understood just this much.

If you had bound sticky (difficult) karma, the results will be sticky also. Such karmas unfold to give you the opportunity to be free from this stickiness. Everything is your own account. If a person starts cursing you, is his conduct improper? No, this is exactly correct, it is the effect. Whatever it is, it is a worldly interaction, a cause–effect relationship. The difference between the one who knows the Self and the one who is ignorant of the Self is this: The one, who knows the Self, would be glad if someone were to insult him because he sees that this is freeing him from the karma. A person, who does not know the Self, will retaliate and bind more karma. When someone insults you, it is nothing but the effect of your own karma and he just happens to be instrumental in it. With this awareness, new karma is not bound. Every effect, karma brings with it its own *nimit* (instrument). It has already been decided through which 'instrument', the effect will occur. *Dharma* is where there is no attachment or abhorrence during the karma effect.

Are Obstacles Self-Created?

Questioner: If someone tries to stop us from coming to *satsang*, is it because of our own karma?

Dadashri: Yes. Nobody can touch you if you are not at fault. Everything you experience is the result of your own mistakes. You yourself have bound these karmas of obstacles. And karmas that have been created will have to be experienced.

Questioner: Were these mistakes made in our previous life?

Dadashri: Yes, in the past life.

Questioner: Although I interact nicely with a person,

he speaks in a hurtful manner and behaves badly. Is that from the past life?

Dadashri: What do karmas of the past life mean? It means that they were created in the form of a 'plan'. This plan, the cause, is one's inner intent. These karmas are discharging now and one has no choice but to experience them.

Conflicts Between Husband And Wife...

The bedbugs and mosquitoes that bite are far better and far less troublesome than the husbands and wives that bite each other. Do you agree that husbands and wives bite one another?

Questioner: Yes. They do bite.

Dadashri: Then this biting must stop. The bedbugs go away after biting. The poor thing will leave you alone after it has had its portion. The wife however, goes on biting incessantly. One poor man came to me complaining that his wife kept on biting him like a snake. The foolish man! Firstly, why did he get married and secondly, why to a snake? Would that not make him a snake also? Female snakes do not just happen to come along, unless there is a male around.

Questioner: It must be written in his karma and therefore he has to suffer his wife's sting. His wife is not at fault here.

Dadashri: That is it. All this suffering is related to karma. That is why one gets such a wife, husband and mother-in-law etc. There are plenty of good wives, husbands, and mothers-in-law, in the world. Why is it that you are stuck with the one that bites?

Some men constantly quarrel with the wives. The fools do not realize that the suffering is because of their own karma. People always blame the 'instrument'. The wife is merely an 'instrument'. Why do you keep biting the 'instrument'? You will not accomplish anything by doing that. Instead you will go to a lower life form. People have no idea about the type of life form in store for them, so they remain insensitive. If they were told that in their next life they will acquire four legs and a tail (animal life) they would shape up right away.

Questioner: Whose karma is worse, the husband's or the wife's, when fighting with one another?

Dadashri: The one who suffers more. Who will give up the fight?

Questioner: Neither of them will. They will simply carry on fighting.

Dadashri: Then they both have bad karmas. It all happens out of ignorance.

Questioner: If there is understanding then there is no suffering, right?

Dadashri: There is no suffering at all, if they understand. If a child were to throw a stone at you, you would be furious and chase him, would you not? But whom would you get angry with if a stone were to fall on you and injure you badly? Who would you quarrel with?

Questioner: No one.

Dadashri: Similarly, when someone hits you, he is merely an 'instrument'. It is only because one does not have this awareness, that he becomes upset. There would be no suffering if he were to understand the role of an 'instrument' (*nimit*).

Receive Happiness By Giving Happiness

If you plant a cactus, you cannot expect it to bear mangoes. You get the fruit of the tree you plant. In the same way, the consequence of the karma you have to suffer depends on the type of karma that was bound in the first place. If you hurt someone, that person will bear a grudge against you and will vow to take revenge when the opportunity arises. People will take revenge, so do not do any karmas that make people unhappy. If it is happiness that you seek, then you must give happiness and not sorrow to others.

What should you do if someone insults you? Just accept it. He is merely returning what you gave in the past life. If you want more of the abuse, then retaliate, but understand that when it is returned, you will not be able to bear it. So accept whatever comes to you.

There is no injustice in this world. This world has not been unjust, even for a second. That is why nobody will bother you if you stay within your limits. Accept whatever comes your way, as the settlement of your past account.

Discord Is Not Karma Effect

It can only be said that you truly understand when there is no discord in the home. There are no arguments and no differences of opinion. Discord is rampant nowadays. How can you call that living? Even primitive people live better lives than that.

Questioner: But isn't discord bound to happen because of one's unfolding of effect karma?

Dadashri: No, discord does not occur because of effect karma. It arises because of ignorance. Whenever discord occurs, new seeds of karma are being sown. Effect karma does not contain discord. It is because of ignorance that one does not know how to conduct himself, so discord is brought on.

If I were to receive news about the death of a close friend, right away I would analyze it through Gnan the reasons for this news, and then there would be no need for me to suffer any discord. Ignorance however, will bring on discord and despair.

Therefore, discord means ignorance. All discord arises out of ignorance. When ignorance goes, discord disappears.

One should know what everything is all about. Ordinarily, if a child breaks a clay pot, nobody says anything, but when a china cup is broken, everyone gets upset. Why? It is because the clay pot had no value to it. In other words we only create problems when something is valuable to us. We do not create any problems where things do not have any value. Both of the vessels break on account of unfolding of effect karma. Yet we care less for the devalued clay pot.

When a person suffers a loss of two thousand rupees, he suffers mental anguish, while another person who suffers the same loss, will recognize that it happened because of his effect karma. This sort of understanding, will bring everything to a close, otherwise there will be discord. There is no discord in the karmas from previous life. Discord is the fruit of today's ignorance.

Some people remain unperturbed even if their warehouse burns down and they do not have any insurance. They would appear tranquil both on the outside and inside, while some display panic and fear inside and out. That is all ignorance and lack of understanding. The warehouse was destined to burn. Nothing new is happening. No matter how much you punish yourself, nothing would have changed the outcome.

Questioner: Should we calmly accept the outcome of anything?

Dadashri: Yes. You must take everything positively. And you can only see the positive in any situation if you have Gnan. If not, the intellect (*buddhi*), which always looks at the negative, will takeover. The whole world suffers. Everyone thrashes around like fish out of water. How can you call this living? There is a need to understand the art of living. Not everyone achieves liberation, but one should at least know the art of living.

Why Blame The Postman For The Letter With Bad News?

The misery in this world today is due to lack of understanding. It is self-created because of the lack of vision. When one is burnt by fire, he would say that it was not done deliberately, but instead, by mistake. Similarly all misery is based on mistakes. All these miseries are the result of our mistakes. Once the mistakes are gone, the misery will be over.

Questioner: Is that why we have to suffer the misery, because of our karmas?

Dadashri: They are all karmas that we had created, which is why the mistake is our own. No one else is at fault. Others are only 'instruments'. The misery is all yours, but it comes your way through your 'instruments'. Would you hit the postman (instrument) if he were to bring you the telegram informing you of your father's death?

Accounts Of Previous Lives

Questioner: Do we encounter our family members and relatives because of our connections with them in our previous life?

Dadashri: True. There is nothing without connections. They are all accounts. Either we have pushed them around or they have pushed us around. If you have obliged them in the past, then the effect will be sweet. But if you have pushed them around it will be bitter.

Questioner: If someone pushes me around and hurts me, is the suffering I feel the fruit of my karma?

Dadashri: Yes, these are all accounts. He will continue to do so as long as there is an account. The trouble he gives you depends on the extent of your account. Do these chili peppers give you problems?

Questioner: Yes, they do.

Dadashri: They burn in the mouth. That is exactly how it all is. It is the *pudgal* (the body complex) that pushes you around, not the pure Self. The pure Self is simply aware that it is the body that is doing it. It is not the chilies that make us suffer, but that the fault is of the person who eats them, the sufferer. The peppers themselves are in their own natural state. The sufferer is in the unnatural state ("I am Chandulal.").

Questioner: What should we do if we push or shove someone and it hurts him?

Dadashri: You must do *pratikraman* (apology). You have to keep your clothes clean, don't you? You cannot keep them dirty. Ultimately your behavior should be clean as well; it should be such that it does not hurt anyone, even slightly. If someone gets hurt and you do *pratikraman*, you will progress towards liberation.

Can Anyone Take On Another's Misery?

Questioner: Two years ago a renowned saint was in a hospital suffering a terrible sickness. I asked him why all this was happening to him and he told me that it was because he had taken upon himself the miseries of many people. Can anybody do such a thing?

Dadashri: No one can take someone else's misery. These are all excuses for him so that people would continue to worship him as a saint. It was all a result of his own causes. He was simply trying to promote himself. How can anyone who does not even have the strength to evacuate his bowels at will, take on someone else's misery?

Questioner: Even I don't believe that. Miseries cannot be taken away.

Dadashri: Of course not! He is simply making fools out of people, so that he would be worshipped. It is impossible for anyone to take away another's pain. I tell it to their faces that they are suffering their own miseries. What nonsense!

Questioner: But you can make someone miserable, can't you?

Dadashri: One cannot take anyone else's misery. Whatever misery people give you is your own effect. The ability to give and the ability to receive are both effects. Effect means that nobody does it; it just happens!

Miseries Because Of Demerit Karma

Questioner: When a person dies from some kind of disease, people say it is because of bad karma from his past life. Is that true?

Dadashri: Yes, with bad karma you get disease and if there is no bad karma there is no disease. Have you ever come across a person with a disease?

Questioner: My mother died of cancer about two months ago.

Dadashri: It all happens because of bad karma coming into effect. Cancer occurs when *paap* karmas come into effect. All these heart attacks occur because of bad karma. People today bind nothing but *paap* karma. That is their business. All day long, they bind *paap* karma! They do this because they are not aware of it. If they were, they would not do so.

Questioner: Her entire life was spent doing devout religious worship, so why did she get cancer?

Dadashri: The fruits of her worship are yet to come. She will receive that in her next life. This is the fruit of her past life. By sowing good seeds today, you will receive good fruits in your next life.

Questioner: If disease is because of karma, then why does medicine cure it?

Dadashri: Yes, certain diseases are results of bad karmas created in ignorance, so medicine can cure them. If they were intentionally done then there would not be any kind of medicine that would help cure the disease. In both cases one does not go unpunished. The only difference is that the bad karma created in ignorance will receive some kind of help, whereas those done deliberately, will not.

The Result Of Troubling Others

Questioner: What kind of karma causes the physical happiness or unhappiness we experience?

Dadashri: Many people kill and torture cats and dogs unintentionally. When they cause misery to these animals they are not aware of the consequences they will have to face. Killing kittens and puppies and dissecting frogs, has its repercussions. Whatever you do will come back at you. These are all your own 'echoes' (effect).

Questioner: So the pain given to other bodies will be reflected in the same way?

Dadashri: Yes. That is it. The slightest misery you give to any living being will return to your own body.

Questioner: Would a person not be in a state of ignorance when he dissects and cuts all these animals? Does he still have to suffer even though he does not have feelings of animosity toward his victims?

Dadashri: If by accident your hand falls on burning charcoal, you will suffer the consequences. So nobody lets you off, whether it is in ignorance or with awareness, knowingly or unknowingly. Only the suffering is different. All these people suffer because of their own accounts. That is why the Lord has told us to practice *ahimsa* (non-violence) through the mind, body, and speech. If you want to be happy, then you must not hurt any living being, even slightly.

Questioner: Then should a *mahatma* (person who has received Atma Gnan) not become a doctor?

Dadashri: Whether to be a doctor or not is a different matter. It will continue to happen according to one's *prakruti* (inherent nature). His intent should be non-violence so in his next life, he will not have a career in medicine. How can anyone who has the intent not hurt anyone in the slightest, kill even a frog?

Questioner: But on the other hand, he is helping people by caring for them. It benefits people.

Dadashri: That is the way the world functions. It is relative. You cannot call it a benefit.

What Kind Of Karma Does A Mentally Handicapped Person Bind?

Questioner: A normal person would have all kinds of thoughts. Within a minute he would have numerous thoughts and bind many karmas in the process. But a person who is mentally slow never understands a thing. He would be innocent because he has nothing.

Dadashri: Both bind karmas according to their level of understanding. The one who has understanding will create karma with understanding. The one without understanding will bind karma without understanding. His reaction to effect is naïve and more like an animal. If such a person is provoked even slightly, he may even throw a stone at you.

Questioner: Should we not have pity towards these kinds of people?

Dadashri: You must. You should have compassion for such human beings who do not understand. You should help them. His mental problems make him person the way he is. It is not his fault. Even if he hurts you, you should not have bad feelings towards him. You should feel compassion for such a person.

Which Karma Makes One Rich Or Poor?

If one accepts that whatever happens is justice, then he will attain liberation.

Questioner: Then Dada, don't you think that if a poor man who is very virtuous and religious were to see a wealthy man who is devious and immoral, he would be put off by religion all together? He will think that all his piousness has not improved his poverty at all.

Dadashri: Not every religious person is miserable. Perhaps even five percent are happy.

Whatever misery befalls us today is the result of our karma. The fact that a person enjoys wealth and prosperity today is all the result of his karma. He will suffer the consequences of whatever bad deeds he does in this life, in his next life. We will enjoy the fruit of the good deeds we do today, in the next life.

Questioner: Dada, what you are saying is true. But looking at it from the point of worldly interaction, if a man lives in a hut, suffering hunger and thirst, along side a man that lives in a palace, don't you think it would make him angry to see the man in the palace living a life of corruption while he, an honest and decent man cannot even feed his children? How would he be able to remain calm?

Dadashri: The misery that he is experiencing now, is a result of the 'test' (cause) he took in the past life. The other person had also taken the 'test', he passed and now he is receiving the result. Now in this life the rich man's karmas are such that he is going to fail the test of this life and the result will come in the next life. The poor man is now being tested in this life, he will pass the test and he will enjoy its effects in the next life.

Questioner: But until the poor man is able to accept his lot in life, how can he understand that?

Dadashri: He can never accept it. On the contrary he binds more *paap*. He has to know that it is the result of his own karma.

We Do Good But The Reward Is Bad

Questioner: If the consequence of our doing good is bad, does it mean that the bad karmas that we did in our previous life, have cancelled the effect of the good karma?

Dadashri: Yes, they do. If we plant corn and it thrives and grows tall, then when our bad karmas come to fruition, and the last rainfall does not come, the crop withers away. But if our *punya* (merit karma) is strong enough, the corn will mature into a good crop. That is why you must do good karma. Otherwise, look for liberation. Take one of the paths. Either find a way out of this world or do good karmas forever. But humans cannot do good karmas forever. They will undoubtedly end up on a wrong path. They will always encounter bad company.

Questioner: What is the 'thermometer' for recognizing good karma and bad karma?

Dadashri: When good karmas come into effect, we feel good and the atmosphere is peaceful. And when the bad karmas come into effect, we feel uneasy and uncomfortable.

What Goes With You After Death?

Questioner: Does one have to experience the results of good and bad karma, when he takes on another life?

Dadashri: He has to experience it there in the next life. At the time of death, the *Shuddhatma* (the pure Self) goes there into the next life. Along with the Self go the good and bad karmas in the form of a plan, which is called the 'causal body.' The subtle body, which is the electrical body, also follows. All these accompany the Self. Nothing else goes with it.

Questioner: Does one receive human birth over and over or is there also a birth perhaps in another life form?

Dadashri: One goes to every life form from here. As of now about seventy percent of humans here, will go to the animal kingdom.

Therefore from the human form, one can go into the animal form, to celestial form or even to hell and then back into the human form. He becomes whatever he binds (causes). People nowadays bind karmas worthy of the animal life, do they not?

Questioner: Many are doing animal-like karmas indeed.

Dadashri: Their 'reservations' have already been made and the 'tickets' have been issued. What is the point of criticizing those who cheat, lie, and exploit others when they have already got their passage to the animal kingdom booked and confirmed?

Aimless Wandering In The Four Life Forms

Questioner: Do humans go to a lower life form?

Dadashri: From the human form they can even go to the celestial form and become one of the topmost *devas*. And if they go lower, they may even end up in the worst, most hated place possible.

It is only in the human form that one binds karmas. No other life forms bind karmas. In other life forms they only experience the effects of their karma. In the human form, one causes new karmas and also experiences effects of past karmas. He does both. And that is why it is possible for a person to go to any of the four major life forms. These are: celestial, human, animal, and hellish life forms. The cows and all other animals we see and the *devas* too, only experience the karma effects. They do not bind karmas.

Questioner: But humans for the most part do not do good karmas.

Dadashri: The present time cycle, which is characterized by evil and despair, is rampant with generally bad karma.

Questioner: So here new karmas are being bound?

Dadashri: They are being bound day and night. One keeps binding new ones and experiencing the old ones.

Questioner: Is there a better life than this anywhere else?

Dadashri: Nowhere. This is as good as it gets. There are two directions of progress from here. Here if you have a debt, which means that you have bound bad karma; you would have to go to the animal kingdom to pay it off. If your debt were excessive, you would have to take birth in hell, and settle it there before you return to the human life. If you accomplish good karmas here, then you become a more elevated human being and live an entire life of happiness. When that is over, you will either return to the same state or go into the celestial form, where you will enjoy the benefits of your credits. Once the credit is used up, you end up back here in the human form.

Questioner: Is the human lifespan longer than any other life form's?

Dadashri: No, not at all. The celestial beings have a lifespan of a hundred thousand years.

Questioner: You will have to finish all your karmas first before you get a chance to become a celestial being, is that not so?

Dadashri: No, it is nothing like that. If someone is a superhuman then he will definitely become a celestial being. A superhuman is someone who instead of enjoying his own happiness gives it away to others. Such people go to the celestial level.

Questioner: How can you give happiness to others when you yourself are not happy?

Dadashri: That is the reason why you cannot do that. There are however some rare people, but these are a very few and far between. In past eras four to five percent of the human population attained celestial levels. In this era two to four in ten million go there. In this era, you are wise if you do not give misery to others. If you don't give misery to others, you will come back to the human level, into a wealthy family with all the material comforts. Here again one begins the process of binding karmas, through cheating and stealing, becoming worthy of a bestial life form.

Questioner: Then what law governs this cycle?

Dadashri: The one who is destined for lower life forms does not get caught for his bad deeds. But the person destined for higher life forms gets arrested for the smallest offence. In this way, he is stopped immediately and his coming life changes, before he gets on the wrong path.

Who does nature assist? Nature helps the heavy karmas become heavier and the light karmas become lighter. The lighter ones rise to a higher life form and the heavier ones sink to the lower life forms. That is the law of nature. The one who has never stolen before gets caught as soon as he steals for the first time, whereas the hardcore thief never gets caught because his karmas are heavy.

Only Humans Bind Karma

Questioner: Is there another life form other than the human where less karmas are bound?

Dadashri: There is no binding of karma in other life forms. It is only here in the human life that karmas are being bound. Moreover, in places where no karmas are being charged, they ask, "Why are we in this prison?" A place where karmas are bound is actually called freedom, because here there is a choice. The other three levels are all 'jails' because there is no choice.

Questioner: Is it only in the human life form that karmas are bound, including the good ones?

Dadashri: Both good and bad karmas are bound here.

The humans bind karma. If they cause harm or misery to people, they go to the animal form or a life in hell. If their karmas give happiness to others then they return to the human life or go to the celestial level. So the life level depends on the type of karma bound. Once the level is decided, one has to go through that level, experience the effects and return to the human form.

Only humans have the right to bind karma, no one else. Those who have this right must wander through all the four life forms. If they do not do karmas at all, not an iota of cause-karma, they are liberated from this cycle. One can attain liberation only in the human form. There is no other place from which one can attain liberation. Have you ever seen anybody not doing any karma?

Questioner: No, I have not.

Dadashri: All these animals you see, they all eat, and drink and fight and still they do not bind karmas. Likewise, it is possible for a human being not to bind any karma while living. This happens when they do not become the docrs of the karma and remain as the sufferer of past karmas. When they come to me and receive this knowledge of Self-realization, they become free from all doership of karma and thereafter only the experiencing of previously created karma remains. The ego is the doer of karma.

The Balance Of Eight Lifetimes

Questioner: Whenever a living being goes into a life

form where it does not bind karma but simply goes through the discharge effects of karma, how does that living being acquire the next life?

Dadashri: There is a vast area. When a human leaves from here, he may reincarnate as a cow and experience the life of a cow, after which he may be born as a goat. It is not definite that he will be a goat. It can be anything depending on his account. It depends on the causes. He may even be born as a donkey. After two hundred years or so of such wandering and paying off the debt from his karmas, he takes birth again in the human form. Anywhere else, other than the human level, one is transported from one life form to another without cause karma. The process of taking different life forms is from the causes created in the human life form. The discharge may happen in a variety of other life forms and it is not necessary to return to the human life level. It happens because all the karmas have been experienced. These causes are in the form of layers. One layer is shed (effect) in each subsequent life form. When all the layers are gone and eight lives have been completed, he then comes back to the human form. At the most it takes eight lives of wandering about in other life forms before one can return to the human life. That is the law of nature.

The balance of karma worthy of the human form stays with him, wherever he goes, even if he goes to the celestial form. It is because of this balance that he is able to return to the human form. Keeping aside this balance, all other karmas are discharged through experience.

Questioner: After returning to the human form, how does his life function? Does it function on his *bhaavs* (causes from last human life)? Based on what karma does his life function now?

Dadashri: He has with him a balance of human karmas. The balance is there, but if a debt is incurred (bad karma), then you have to go and take care of it before you can return. If one has acquired a credit, then he must experience that before returning. The balance remains with you and it never gets used up. When does it get used up? It is used up when the 'doership' goes away. Only then can you be liberated. The doership will never go away unless the ego goes. The ego is the doership. If the ego is there, you experience your karmas elsewhere and return back to where you were before.

Questioner: Upon returning to the human form from other life forms, where do you take birth? For example, are you born as a fisherman or a king?

Dadashri: Your life resumes at the level you were at when you left the last human form to pay your debts or to enjoy your credits. This is just like returning home after completing all the necessary shopping. In the same way, the human life is the home. You have to come home. And when the ego comes to an end, you do not even have to stay in this world. Liberation happens when the ego stops. The ego is not used in any other life forms. In the experience of the effect karma, the ego is not used and so no karmas are bound. The cows and oxen do not have egos. A horse may appear to have an ego, but it is the ego that is being discharged, it is not a true ego. It is because of the ego that you are here. When it is gone, you will be liberated.

A Return Ticket From The Animal Kingdom

Questioner: You say that one receives the fruit of his karma. So then, can these animals come back into the human form?

Dadashri: They are the ones who come here. They are the ones that are here now. Their population has increased. And they are the ones engaged in unscrupulous enterprises.

Questioner: What kind of good karma have these animals done that they are born into the human form?

Dadashri: They do not have to do good karmas. Let me explain to you. A man falls into a debt and becomes bankrupt. People say that he is ruined. Once he clears his debts, would they go on saying that he is bankrupt?

Questioner: No, then they would not say that.

Dadashri: In the same way, you go from here to the animal form to clear your debts and return, or may go to the celestial level to clear your credits and return.

Making A Reservation For Lower Life Levels

Questioner: How can we tell that a human will only be born in the animal form?

Dadashri: All his attributes and qualities will be evident. He will have beastly thoughts, thoughts of how to cheat and deprive others. At the time of his death, his appearance will be bestial.

Questioner: If we were to plant the seed of a mango, we would get a mango tree. Does this apply to humans also? Will humans be humans in the next life?

Dadashri: Yes, back to a human form means, that if you look in a maternity ward it is not puppies that are born to a woman. Do you understand that? If a person is virtuous and has good thoughts, he will indeed return to the human form. If instead of enjoying the things that he is entitled to, he gives them to others, he is a superhuman and he will go to celestial life form. There is nothing wrong with one enjoying his own wife, because he is married to her. A person cannot take pleasure in things that are not his. Even thoughts about such things themselves are an indication that his next life will be in the animal form. That is his visa for going there.

Questioner: The law of karma is such that a human has to experience the fruits of his karma in a human life.

Dadashri: No. The effect of past cause karma must be experienced here and here only. Thoughts due to inner intent of depriving others, stealing from others, cheating others and negative decisions of hurting and depriving others, will take one to the other life forms. The karmas created as cause in one's past life have to be experienced here only. The effect of beastly behavior will be experienced here. How does one experience it? The experience is in the form of a public insult or criticism. This effect is the effect of the effect. The causes created within by bad thoughts and intentions to harm others will take them to animal life.

Who Is The Sufferer Here?

Questioner: Good deeds bind merit karma and bad deeds bind demerit karma. Who experiences the fruits of this good and bad karma that are created? Is it the body or the Soul?

Dadashri: The doer of the good and bad karma experiences it. The ego binds the karma and the ego experiences the fruit of the karma. Neither the body nor the Self (Soul) experiences it. The ego is the doer and the sufferer. If the ego is with the body ("I am Chandulal,") then the suffering is of the ego only. If the ego is without the body ("I am *Shuddhatma*,"), then also the suffering is of the ego only (discharge ego).

Questioner: Is there such a thing as hell or heaven after death?

Dadashri: After death there is both heaven and hell.

Questioner: So if the karmas are bad, who goes to hell? Does the Self go there?

Dadashri: The body and the Soul are always together.

Questioner: When one dies, is not the body cast off here?

Dadashri: A new body is formed there. The body for hell is formed separately. In hell the body is like mercury.

Questioner: Is it the body that experiences karmas or is it the Self that does?

Dadashri: The ego does. The one that caused the karma for hell, experiences them.

What Kind Of Karma Did Hitler Bind?

Why did Hitler, who murdered so many innocent people, not receive the fruit of his karma? How did all the people that suffered because of him come together in such a way? How did all that come together? Was this an effect? Yes.

Now in the next life, the effect for him will be the hell level. Why? The scriptures have said that those who have died here and those whom the world considers as clearly violent and disreputable, will go to hell or the animal life form. Those who the world respects and worships will go to the celestial levels, or be born as humans again.

Collective Karma Effect

Questioner: Which power is behind these earthquakes and volcanoes?

Dadashri: *Vyavasthit Shakti* (Scientific Circumstantial Evidences). *Vyavasthit shakti* does everything. All the evidences have to be present. All the evidences must be ready. If there is the slightest possible shortcoming in any one of them, then nothing will materialize.

Questioner: These cyclones are also *vyavasthit*?

Dadashri: Then what else produces the cyclones all across Bombay? Many are not aware of it because it does not affect them. Although the cyclone hits everyone in Bombay, it affects people in different ways. Some people's homes get blown away while even the doormats of certain homes remain untouched. Everything happens very methodically and precisely. There is no need to be afraid of the cyclones. *Vyavasthit* sends everything.

Questioner: All these earthquakes, cyclones and wars, don't they happen because of the law of construction-destruction (increase-decrease)?

Dadashri: No. They are all dependent on the timing of karma effect. Everyone is experiencing the consequences of their karma. Earthquakes occur even when there is an increase in the human population in the world. If it were based on an increased destruction, then would it happen?

Questioner: Is it the timing for the individuals who have to suffer it?

Dadashri: It includes everyone, humans, animals, everything. The unfolding of the effect is collective. Just like the effect that came for Hiroshima and Nagasaki.

Questioner: Just as an individual does bad deeds, is the act done collectively, suffered collectively too? If just one person goes to steal and if ten people go on a raid, does that mean they are all punished collectively?

Dadashri: Yes, the punishment is going to be in its entirety but the amount, with the intensity of inner intent of the individuals at that time. Perhaps one of them was forced to steal against his will. The account depends on the strength of the intent. It is very precise.

Questioner: But these natural disasters that occur, for example a cyclone or a volcano that kills thousands of people, would that be as a result of collective punishment?

Dadashri: That is everyone's account. Only the ones th a pending account get caught, nobody else. Say there was an earthquake in Bombay and some folks had gone on vacation to another city while others from elsewhere were here in Bombay. These are all effects of accounts.

Questioner: Many more people die collectively nowadays than in previous times. Before, we never used to witness so many people dying collectively in such large numbers. Is that the result of the collective bad karma they did?

Dadashri: There were not many large groups in the past. Nowadays there are many working under individual flags for example, communism etc., so that all the deeds are grouped together.

Questioner: So are the droughts, floods, and earthquakes killing hundreds of people actually a result for a group?

Dadashri: It is all a result of a group of people's causes.

Questioner: So if they are to be a part of the punishment, they will be drawn here no matter where they are?

Dadashri: Nature brings them here in the area of the earthquake or cyclone etc, and punishes them.

Questioner: Yes, Dada. There are examples of people who have missed a plane for some reason, while others who were not supposed to fly, find themselves on board a plane that crashes.

Dadashri: They are all accounts. Methodical justice. It is absolutely precise. There is no owner of this. If there were, than injustice may occur.

Questioner: Was the Air India plane crash an 'instrument' for all those people? Was it *Vyavasthit?*

Dadashri: Only an account, nothing happens without an account of debit-credit.

A Good Deed Cannot Negate A Bad Deed

Questioner: Is the suffering a net result of the addition and subtraction of bad karma and good karma?

Dadashri: No. Addition and subtraction does not occur, the deeds do not cancel each other out. This has been a rule since the existence of this world. People would take advantage of it if this were the case. The smart people would end up doing a hundred good deeds and ten bad deeds, leaving ninety credits of good deeds. Nature makes sure that both good and bad deeds are experienced.

Questioner: Dada, is it true that when we do any kind of charitable work like building a hospital, the fruit of the other negative karmas we have done will be less intense?

Dadashri: No, it is not reduced. There is no subtraction or addition in the account. New karmas are bound for the good deeds, but one will have to suffer the consequences of harming others. Otherwise all the calculating business-minded people will subtract the bad karmas and keep the profit. It is not like that. Natural law is exact. If you have done any harm, just even once, its fruits will come. Two bad deeds will not be deducted from a hundred good deeds. Both have to be suffered separately.

Questioner: So the fruits of these good karmas and the bad karmas are separate?

Dadashri: The fruits of bad karmas will be bad and the fruit of good karmas will be good. Nothing increases or decreases. What kind of law prevails in nature? Say you do a hundred dollars worth of good karma by donating to a charity, but you also do five dollars worth bad karma by insulting someone. The five dollars will become a debit in your account and the good deed of a hundred dollars will become a credit. The law is very precise.

If this were not so, then all the businessmen would credit-debit all the time and ensure that they had a net credit balance. There would never be any unhappiness and so no one would ever seek liberation, because there would be nothing but good deeds. So the law credits a hundred and loans you five, which is not deducted. You will have to experience whatever credit you accumulate. Excessive credits will bring excessive fruits, which become cumbersome to enjoy. After a while, you will tire from too much of a good thing. Too much credit becomes cumbersome and too much debit also becomes cumbersome. One becomes tired of all the luxuries and wants to revert back to simplicity. This is because whatever comforts they experience is not real, is not the bliss of the Self. Rather, it is imaginary and temporary happiness. One never tires or becomes dissatisfied with the permanent bliss of the Pure Soul.

The Path Of Liberation From The Bondage Of Karma

Questioner: How can we be free of the karmas bound in the previous lives? We have some notion that we are here because of good and bad karmas in our past life. How can we find a solution to the problem?

Dadashri: Now if someone bothers you, you should understand that you must have done something bad to him in your past life, and now he is returning the favor. So you must resolve the situation calmly and peacefully. But because you cannot remain peaceful, you end up sowing new seeds of karma. There is only one way to deal with karmas bound from the previous life and that is through peace and equanimity. You should not have a single bad thought about other people. You should simply feel that you are experiencing your account and that whatever the person may be doing to you is all on account of your own karma. You should understand that you are suffering because of your own previous bad deeds. Only then is there any freedom. As a matter of fact, he is giving you such a difficult time because of the unfolding effect of your own karma: he is simply an 'instrument'. All the troublemakers of this world are merely 'instruments'. Even he that steals a hundred dollars from you in the street is an 'instrument'. It is your own account. Why is it that you were awarded the prize and not someone else?

The Importance Of Prayer While Suffering Karma

Questioner: Dada, what I want to know is if the effect of karma can be changed through prayer?

Dadashri: The effect of karma is composed of parts. One aspect is such that it can be eliminated with prayer. A second type can be eliminated with a little spiritual effort. The third type is the one that no matter how strong the spiritual effort, there is no escape from the suffering. It is too sticky.

Questioner: But even if the karmas are very sticky, doesn't prayer make a difference?

Dadashri: It makes no difference. Although at the time of praying, there may be some peace.

Questioner: Does one get the strength to experience the fruits of the karmas by praying?

Dadashri: No. The misery is the effect on you. With prayer, you can experience a portion of happiness in misery. But it is difficult for the prayer to remain continuously. When situations are bad and the mind is spoiled it is hard to keep praying. If it is possible to keep praying, it would be the ideal thing and one should do it by recalling and remembering 'Dada', who himself is free from his body. If you recall the one who is not attached to his body and then say the prayers, the prayer will stay, otherwise it will not.

Questioner: Under those circumstances praying does not come to mind.

Dadashri: It would not come to mind. One's awareness would disappear and his ability to remember would be gone too.

The Binding Of Vows To Deva-Devis

Questioner: Does one bind karmas for making any kind of vows to any *deva-devis* (celestial bodies)?

Dadashri: Certainly karmas are bound when a vow is taken. By doing so we ask them to do something for us. They may even oblige us, by doing something. We give them something in return, which is why we bind karma.

Questioner: By staying with a saint, can one be freed from binding karma?

Dadashri: The binding of karmas is reduced. You will bind karmas of merit, and this does not hurt you. The karma of demerit is not bound.

Awareness Against The Binding Of Karma

Questioner: What can one do to prevent the creation of karma?

Dadashri: If you have bad thoughts or negativity, you should immediately confess them to God. The thoughts will linger as long as there is an account. Just confess to God that you have had bad thoughts and that you are asking for forgiveness and vow never to do it again.

Questioner: If someone commits a murder and then repents in front of God, how can that person be freed from that karma?

Dadashri: Yes, he can be freed. But if he feels contentment after killing, then he will bind very serious bad karma and if he repents for his actions, he will bind a light karma.

Questioner: So regardless of what he does, he still binds karma?

Dadashri: They are bound and then released. The murder that takes place is really a karma that discharges its effect to become free. When does the binding occur? It is bound at the time when the thought enters one's mind that it is okay to kill. At that time a new karma is bound. If while the karma is discharging, he repents, then he can escape its consequences of effect. Killing will have grave consequences. The killer will be disgraced and even suffer all kinds of disease within the body (effect of effect). Everything will have to be suffered here and here only. The new karmas that are bound will not be very sticky, when he repents sincerely. The process of killing is karma effect and it has to be suffered. One must accept the fruit of karma, but if repentance is done whole-heartedly, then the new karma will become light. If the killing is done with enthusiasm then the newly bound karma will be very grave.

A man is forced to kill a deer to feed his family. By killing he commits a bad karma. A prince on the other hand, goes deer hunting for sport and is thrilled when he manages to kill a deer. Now in both situations a deer has been killed. One kills for food and the other for his enjoyment. The man who kills for food will end up from the human form into the animal form! The prince however, who does not eat the meat, but hunts for sport and pleasure, will go to hell. The karma was the same for both but their intentions were different. People are not aware of these rules, so they need someone like me to explain it to them.

Does The Judge Bind Karma For Giving A Death Sentence?

A high court judge was in a dilemma over how he could issue a death sentence after taking Gnan (The knowledge of the Self). I asked him what would happen if he did not. He said that if he gave it, he would be committing a sin.

I showed him a way to deal with his dilemma. I told him that he should be repentant and tell God, "Dear Lord, what did I do to be in this position to sentence someone to death. Please forgive me." He should do *pratikraman* sincerely and then continue to do his work according to the laws of the land.

Questioner: If we seriously injure someone and then do *pratikraman*, don't we bind karma?

Dadashri: You should keep doing *pratikraman* in his name. The amount of *pratikraman* that you do should be equal to the pain you caused him. All you have to do is *pratikraman*; you are not responsible for anything else.

If you do *pratikraman* for any of your actions, seventy five percent of the effect of that act is dissolved. The other twenty-five percent remains like the image of a burnt rope. In the next life, it will disintegrate easily. Every cause has an effect. By doing *pratikraman*, karmas can be shaken off in the next life.

Are Karmas Bound Or Released Through Chanting And Penance?

Questioner: When we do chanting and practice penance, do we bind karmas or do we release ourselves from them?

Dadashri: Karmas are bound. Karmas are bound in everything. Even in sleep you bind karmas. When you do chanting or penance, you bind heavy merit karmas, for which you will receive material happiness in the next life.

Questioner: So how much strength does religion (good deeds) have to free you from karma?

Dadashri: *Dharma* and *adharma* (good and bad deed) are both effects of karma. They keep you bound in the world. If you know the science, karmas can be destroyed immediately. With *dharma* (religion, morality) *punya* karmas are bound and with *adharma* (non-religion, immorality) *paap* karmas are bound. With Atma Gnan (knowledge of the Pure Self) however, karmas are destroyed and burnt to ashes.

Questioner: If one is discharging both the good and the bad, then how can it be called *dharma*?

Dadashri: With *dharma*, karmas of *punya* are bound and with *adharma*, karmas of *paap* are bound. What would you do if someone were to slap you? Would you not slap him back? Double the number and give him back. It is because the unfolding of your effect karma that the man slapped you. He is simply the 'instrument'. Just accept it as a return of your debt and deposit it. Do not give it back. If you do not want to repeat this scene in the next life do not give it back.

The State Of Doership And Non-doership

Questioner: I believe that anytime you do something wrong, you bind karma.

Dadashri: Then do you not also bind karmas for good deeds?

Questioner: Both good and bad deeds, bind karma, right?

Dadashri: You are binding karmas, right at this very moment. At the present time you are binding karmas of very high merit. But there will never be a day when you don't bind karmas at all. Why is that?

Questioner: We are always engaged in some form of activity, whether it is good or bad.

Dadashri: Yes, but should there not be a way by which no karmas are bound? How did Lord Mahavir manage to liberate himself without binding karmas? As long as you have this body, you will bind karmas. Do you not have to do certain kinds of activity, such as going to the toilet?

Questioner: Yes, the fruits of the karmas that were bound have to be experienced.

Dadashri: As long as you are binding karmas, there will always be a next birth for you. If you bind karmas, you will have to experience the effects in the next life, but doesn't the fact that Lord Mahavir did not have to take another birth, proves that there has to be a way where despite doing daily activities, no new karmas are bound?

Questioner: There must be.

Dadashri: Do you ever wish for a state where no new karma is bound? There is a science where despite doing daily activities of life, no new karmas are bound. When you know that science you will be liberated.

Ignorance Is The Obstruction, Not The Karma

Questioner: Is it because of the fruit of our karmas that we attain this life?

Dadashri: Yes, this whole life has to be spent experiencing the fruits of past karmas. New karmas are caused by *raag-dwesh* (attachment-abhorrence). If you do not have attachment or abhorrence there is no new karma.

There is no problem with the karma effect. Karmas will have their effects as long as this body exists. The problem is with attachment and abhorrence. The fully Enlightened Ones tell you to live your life without attachment and abhorrence.

Whatever activity you do in this life has no value. Only when attachment and abhorrence occur a new karma is bound. You are not responsible if attachment or abhorrence do not occur.

From birth to death, this body is an effect. Only the attachment and abhorrence are what binds the account. That is why the *Vitarags* (the fully enlightened Ones) tell us to become *Vitarag* and be liberated.

When someone insults me, I know that he is insulting Ambalal Patel. He insults this body complex. He cannot understand or recognize the Self. I, the Pure Self remain the Knower and the Seer of the event. I am *Vitarag*. I do not have any attachment-abhorrence towards him or towards anything in this world. Final liberation is at hand for me.

The message of the *Vitarags* is that it is not the karmas that obstruct our liberation; it is our ignorance. Ignorance of what? The ignorance of the Self. As long as there is a body, karmas will continue to happen, but when ignorance is gone, the binding of new karma stops.

When Does The Discharge Of Karma Occur?

Questioner: When do karmas stop occurring?

Dadashri: It is when you have the experience of, "I am Pure Self." So when you become the pure Self, you will stop binding karmas. The discharge of karmas will continue until they are completely exhausted.

So how can we stop karmas from binding? Once you come into the nature of the Self, no new karma will bind. This happens when the Gnani Purush makes you aware of your own Pure Self. After that, new karmas do not bind and old karmas continue to discharge. When all the karmas have discharged, you will attain final liberation.

Now do you understand karma? Whenever you become the doer, you bind karma but once you are freed from that doership, you stop binding new karma. When I release you from the doership, you will stop binding new karmas and only the effects of the old karmas remain. These you will have to experience. No new causes will occur; only the effects will remain. And when all the effects have been completely experienced, you will attain final liberation.

Jai Sat Chit Anand

Books of Akram Vignan of Dada Bhagwan

1. Adjust Everywhere
2. Ahimsa : Non-Violence
3. Anger
4. Aptavani - 1
5. Aptavani - 2
6. Aptavani - 4
7. Aptavani - 5
8. Aptavani - 6
9. Aptavani - 8
10. Aptavani - 9
11. Autobiography of Gnani Purush A.M.Patel
12. Avoid Clashes
13. Brahmacharya : Celibacy Attained With Understanding
14. Death : Before, During & After...
15. Flawless Vision
16. Generation Gap
17. Harmony In Marriage
18. Life Without Conflict
19. Money
20. Noble Use of Money
21. Pratikraman : The master key that resolves all conflicts (Abridged & Big Volume)
22. Pure Love
23. Right Understanding to Help Others
24. Science of Karma
25. Science of Speech
26. Shree Simandhar Swami : The Living God
27. The Essence Of All Religion
28. The Fault Is Of the Sufferer
29. The Guru and The Disciple
30. The Practice of Humanity
31. Tri Mantra : The mantra that removes all worldly obstacles
32. Whatever Happened is Justice
33. Who Am I ?
34. Worries

'Dadavani' Magazine is published every month in English

Contact

Dada Bhagwan Parivar

Adalaj : **Trimandir**, Simandhar City, Ahmedabad-Kalol Highway, Adalaj, Dist.: Gandhinagar - 382421, Gujarat, India.
Tel : (079) 39830100, **Email :** info@dadabhagwan.org

Ahmedabad : **Dada Darshan**, 5, Mamtapark Society, B/h. Navgujarat College, Usmanpura, Ahmedabad- 14.
Tel. : (079) 27540408

Vadodara : 1) **Trimandir**, Nr. Babaria College, Vadodara-Surat Highway, NH-8, Varnama Village. **Tel. :** 9574001557
2) **Dada Mandir**, 17, Mama ni Pol (Street), Opp. Raopura Police Station, Salatvada, Vadodara. **Cell. :** 9924343335

Rajkot : **Trimandir**, Ahmedabad-Rajkot Highway, Nr. Targhadiya Cross Road, Maliyasan Village, Rajkot. **Cell.:** 9274111393

Bhuj : **Trimandir**, Behind Hill Garden, Airport Road, Near Sahyognagar, Bhuj (Kutch). **Tel. :** (02832) 290123

Anjar : **Trimandir**, Anjar-Mundra Rd, Nr. Sinogra Patiya, Sinogra Village, Ta - Anjar. **Tel. :** 9924346622

Morbi : **Trimandir**, Village-Jepur, Morbi-Navlakhi Road, Morbi, Dist.-Rajkot. **Tel. :** (02822) 297097

Surendranagar : **Trimandir**, Nr. Lok Vidyalaya, Surendranagar-Rajkot Highway, Muli Road, Surendranagar. **Tel. :** 9737048322

Amreli : **Trimandir**, Liliya road bypass chokadi, Kharawadi, Dist - Amreli. **Tel. :** 9924344460

Godhra : **Trimandir**, Village-Bhamaiya, Opp. FCI Godown, Godhra, Dist.-Panchmahal. **Tel. :** (02672) 262300

Mumbai : Dada Bhagwan Parivar, **Cell. :** 9323528901

Bangalore : Dada Bhagwan Parivar, **Cell. :** 9590979099

U.S.A. : **DBVI Tel. :** +1 877-505-DADA (3232),
Email : info@us.dadabhagwan.org

U.K. : **Dada Darshan (UK)** Tel. :+44 330-111-DADA (3232),
Email : info@uk.dadabhagwan.org

Kenya : +254 722 722 063   **Singapore** : +65 81129229
Australia : +61 421127947   **New Zealand :** +64 21 0376434
UAE : +971 557316937   **Germany** : +49 700 32327474

www.dadabhagwan.org